CARING FOR CRITTERS

One Year at a Wildlife Rescue Centre

NICHOLAS READ

Heritage House Publishing Company Ltd.
heritagehouse.ca

Cataloguing information available from Library and Archives Canada
978-1-77203-387-8 (paperback)
978-1-77203-388-5 (ebook)

Copyedited by Nandini Thaker
Cover and interior book design by Setareh Ashrafologhalai
Cover and interior photographs courtesy of Critter Care Wildlife Society

The interior of this book was produced on FSC®-certified, acid-free paper, processed chlorine free, and printed with vegetable-based inks.

Most of the information in this book was collected through personal interviews between the author and staff at the Critter Care Wildlife Society. The views and opinions contained in this book do not necessarily reflect those of the publisher.

Heritage House gratefully acknowledges that the land on which we live and work is within the traditional territories of the Lkwungen (Esquimalt and Songhees), Malahat, Pacheedaht, Scia'new, T'Sou-ke, and W̱SÁNEĆ (Pauquachin, Tsartlip, Tsawout, Tseycum) Peoples.

We acknowledge the financial support of the Government of Canada through the Canada Book Fund (CBF) and the Canada Council for the Arts, and the Province of British Columbia through the British Columbia Arts Council and the Book Publishing Tax Credit.

25 24 23 22 21   1 2 3 4 5

Printed in China

*To Dr. Andrew Howard, for your
patience, your wisdom, your willingness
to listen, and above all your belief
that everything will work out in the end.*

CONTENTS

NOTE: This book contains information about injured, sick, and orphaned wildlife, including some stories about animals that are injured because of their perceived threat to humans and some stories about animals that have had to be put down. Some of the content in this book may be upsetting to younger or more sensitive readers.

INTRODUCTION

CRITTER CARE. Cute name. Fitting, too, given how adorable its critters are. Have you ever seen a baby raccoon, a week-old fawn, or a bear cub? Cute doesn't begin to cover it. In the flesh—or fur—they are turn-yourself-inside-out cute. Too cute to be true. Cute with a capital C.

But when you have to look after almost 1,800 critters a year, cute only goes so far. You also have to be dedicated, selfless, immensely hard-working, and tireless. A touch of heroism helps, too. In spring, when the Critter Care Wildlife Society, a wildlife rehabilitation centre in Langley, British Columbia (on unceded Kwantlen traditional territory), is brimming with orphaned pups, cubs, and kits, staff and volunteers often work twelve to fourteen hours a day. The babies must be fed regularly, several times a day, day after day, for weeks, and there's no shirking it. It has to be done, or the pups, cubs, and kits will die. It's that straightforward.

But that's what Critter Care is about. Looking after animals who would perish if they were left motherless, sick or injured, and alone in the wild. There are other wildlife rehab centres in BC, but Critter Care is special in that its primary focus is mammals (though it would never refuse to treat any other kind of animal too; it once looked after a turtle named Scarlet). Most other rehab centres focus on birds, making Critter Care the only

Critter Care founder and executive director Gail Martin has run the wildlife rescue organization since 1994, when she and her husband, Richard, took over the five-acre (0.4-hectare) rural property in Langley, BC, from the local regional government. Since then she and her staff and interns have looked after tens of thousands of orphaned, injured, and sick animals.

wildlife rehab centre in southern BC to concentrate its care on raccoons, rabbits, squirrels, coyotes, bears, deer, opossums, beavers, porcupines, mink, and more. It's even had a couple of bobcats pass through its gate as well as one cougar. (The Northern Lights Wildlife Shelter in northern BC is similar in that it also specializes in the rescue of bears, including grizzlies. It also cares for moose and deer.)

Run by its founder, Gail Martin, it takes seven staff, including her, more than 100 volunteers, and about 50 interns to keep Critter Care going and the animals it looks after alive. Interns are volunteers who actually live at the centre as part of a work/ education program. They fly in from all over the world—Europe, Asia, Australia, and the USA—to spend up to a year living in a dorm on the five-acre (0.4-hectare) field in a forest and learning about the animals they care for. They pay their own airfare, but once they arrive, they get their room, board, and laundry free.

Most are in their twenties—many are university students—but not all. One of the best interns Martin ever had was a 67-year-old woman from California who spent eight weeks living on the society's grounds in her camper. In other words, it's not just the animals who have to be fed. Interns are essential to Critter Care—it literally couldn't manage without them—so the cost of their keep is one of the reasons it takes $1 million a year to keep Critter Care going. And all of it comes from donations. It receives no government funding, but people and even some companies are generous, Gail says, so somehow the money is found.

There has been a Critter Care in Langley since 1984, but it didn't begin where it is now. It started life in a spare bedroom in Gail's house. Before then, Gail, a lifelong lover of animals who fed peanut butter sandwiches to the raccoons who came to her parents' door, had volunteered for five years at a wildlife rehab centre in Surrey that took in birds and mammals. But she didn't like the way the woman who ran the place treated the mammals. She believed she gave them short shrift compared to the birds. So Gail's husband, Richard, suggested she open a mammal rehab centre of her own.

Richard Martin died in 2011, but he lives in Gail's heart every day. Without him, she says, there never would have been a Critter Care.

Sadly, Richard died in 2011, but he will always be a part of Critter Care, says Gail, because without him there would be no such place. He was literally its inspiration. "I could not have done this without the support of my husband," she says with a passion her husband always admired. "Critter Care would not exist if he didn't believe in me and if he didn't believe I could do it."

The BC provincial government forbids Critter Care from looking after cougars because they are predators and therefore deemed too dangerous. André, a young male, tested that rule one year. However, when it was time for him to be released, the government wouldn't allow it. He had to be transferred to a sanctuary in the US instead.

In that first year, the Martins looked after 300 animals. They reared them if they were orphans or made them well if they were ill or hurt. Then they released them into the wild. Not all of them survived—that's the sad truth of all wildlife rehab centres—but most did. Certainly enough to expand the refuge into the house's garage the next year (when the number of animals they cared for doubled) and eventually, in 1994, to its present premises by a quiet road in Langley, about 50 kilometres (30 miles) southeast of Vancouver.

When the Martins leased the property from the regional government, they took over what had been a horse ranch. But there was no barn, only a house that now serves as Critter Care's triage centre. (Triage is when caregivers decide which animals are in the most urgent need of attention and which ones can wait a while.) There was an old coal stove in a corner of what was once the house's living room, and hanging over it was a dense canopy of soot. But that was it. Talk about humble beginnings.

But it had potential. At least Richard believed it did. He and Gail picked up the key to it on his birthday, November 13, which fell on a Friday that year. Friday the Thirteenth. "We went into the house, and I looked at him and said, 'Oh my God, what have I done?'" Gail recalls. To which Richard, wrapping her in a reassuring hug, replied: "It's Friday the Thirteenth, and it's my birthday, and this will always be a good day for Critter Care." And so it has been. Gail remembers it every year.

The Martins and some of their friends spent the next year refurbishing the house and building a couple of raccoon enclosures. They also continued to care for animals in the garage of the house they lived in, so their days were full, to say the least. But they coped, and over time Critter Care grew.

Today, there are 56 structures on the property, and most of them are animal

The Martins launched Critter Care in a spare bedroom in their house. From there it grew to their garage and finally to where it is now.

enclosures. But even now the place is not finished. It probably never will be. That's because the number of animals Critter Care cares for keeps rising. The main reason for this is stark and simple: As more and more people inhabit the world, more and more of its wilderness is lost to them. Where there were once forests, marshes, and grasslands, there are now office towers, shopping malls, and housing estates. Wild animals are slowly but steadily being squeezed out of the only homes they have.

Compared to some other parts of the world, British Columbia still has vast tracts of wilderness where the kinds of animals Critter Care looks after can continue to roam free. But those areas are shrinking, as industry and development expand and invade. Although the BC government has an environment ministry, it hasn't brought forward many major laws recently to protect animals—other than outlawing grizzly bear hunting in 2017. There are many gaps in how BC treats its wildlife and wild spaces, including allowing some outdated and harmful practices, like hunting wolves to protect caribou. For over two decades, scientists and environmental advocates have been calling for new or updated laws that would better protect endangered species, but progress has been frustratingly slow.

The government does employ "conservation officers" whose duty, you might guess, is to conserve wildlife. In reality, though, the true role of conservation

BOTTOM As this drone photograph shows, there are more than 50 structures built on Critter Care's 0.4-hectare property, and new ones are being built all the time.

officers is to manage conflicts between people and wildlife. This is important in terms of protecting people from dangerous situations with cougars, bears, coyotes, wolves, and other animals. It also stops people from breaking laws against hunting or fishing when and where they're not supposed to, or otherwise harming animals and their habitats. Unfortunately, there is a history of conservation officers acting too quickly with their guns, and many animals are injured, killed, or orphaned as a result.

This is one of the reasons it's so important that organizations like Critter Care exist. They care deeply for and about BC's wildlife, and they literally save their lives.

What follows in the next 12 chapters— one for each month—is a diary of a year in the life of Critter Care, of how it survives and thrives. You'll meet individual animals and hear their stories. You'll also meet some of the people who look after them, because Critter Care is a place where humans and non-humans live closely and compatibly, always on the lookout for each other. As you'll see, it couldn't function any other way.

JUST FOLLOWING ORDERS

IN THIS BOOK you will find many references to an organization called the BC Conservation Officer Service. This is an office of the government that, despite its name, is primarily a law enforcement agency. In other words, the main role of conservation officers (COs) is to enforce and ensure public safety around wild animals. Because of the way the laws were written, officers are legally allowed to shoot and kill wildlife when they perceive it to be a danger to people.

Not only that, if a conservation officer should happen upon a distressed adult coyote, bear, or cougar, he or she must kill it rather than attempt to treat it. Independent organizations like Critter Care are not allowed to care for adult cougars, coyotes, or bears because they are predators and therefore not permitted to be rehabilitated. The one and only time Critter Care was permitted to look after a cougar was in 2007. He was a juvenile male they named André. When he was healed, he could not be re-released into the wild but had to be transferred to a wildlife sanctuary in the US. The government wouldn't allow Critter Care to return him to his home.

Because of the difficult regulations from the government and the fact that so many animals are brought to Critter Care as a result of actions by conservation officers, there is understandably a lot of frustration and tension between the two organizations. In reaction to a public outcry against the continued killing of animals (primarily bears), the BC Conservation Officer Service has begun relocating animals in recent years.

Most of Critter Care's bears are still asleep in January, but unlike true hibernators, bears wake up from time to time, sometimes to do nothing more than stretch their legs.

JANUARY

JANUARY IS USUALLY a quiet month at Critter Care. It will be months before the organization's real work begins: the care and rearing of multitudes of orphaned baby animals, which appear each spring and summer. Of course, staff never know when a distressed animal will need attention. (Sadly, one of the first duties senior wildlife technician Nathan Wagstaffe has to perform this year is to euthanize a skunk critically injured by a car.)

This January is different. Last year at this time, Critter Care was looking after 20 animals. This year, it's caring for 70, including 27 bears. A year ago, it had just three bears. Nathan is at a loss to explain such a drastic leap, but he is very concerned about bears wandering into urban areas, especially if they catch the attention of conservation officers. With the high risk of mother bears being killed after rooting through people's garbage, gardens, and cars, Critter Care is often left to raise the orphaned cubs instead.

Fortunately, 14 of the bears are asleep at the moment, which means they don't require any active care. But the rest don't have enough body fat to snore away the winter, so they remain awake and needy. One of them, a female named Roxxy, weighed only seven kilograms (16 pounds) when she was rescued the day after Christmas, despite having been born last winter. This is possible

Thanks to climate change, it doesn't snow in southwestern BC nearly as much as it used to. But the white stuff still falls now and then, and when it does, it wreaks havoc with Critter Care's plumbing.

because of a baby bear's amazing ability to stop their body from growing bigger, but still remain alive, when there isn't sufficient food to make growth possible.

The rest of the animals, however, are primarily the products of a previously unheard of phenomenon. Last year, and for the first time in Critter Care's history, baby wild animals were being born and orphaned as late as the end of October. Normally, animals stop breeding at the start of September. But last year, for reasons Critter Care can't explain (though climate change is a possible factor), they kept going. As a result, in addition to the bears, Critter Care now has an uncommonly large assortment of otters, beavers, and especially raccoons.

The exception is Dame, short for Dame Judi Dentures. She, too, was rescued late last year, but she is an ancient river otter with front teeth so worn she can barely

These sheds are where the society's raccoons are kept as they're readied for release. That usually happens in the fall, but sometimes a few are held over the winter if staff don't think they're fit to be on their own yet.

chew. All she can eat is the otter equivalent of baby food, and so she will probably remain at Critter Care for the rest of her life.

MID-JANUARY also brings something rare to southwestern BC—snow and sub-zero temperatures. Critter Care is freezing. At least its pipes are. Fortunately, they're still working in the society's main house, so volunteers have to go there to fill buckets with drinking water. The cold is so bad that an adult raccoon found limping by the roadside froze to death before he could receive treatment. Any animals not housed inside are in sheds stuffed with bedding, straw, and heat lamps. The otters' pool is an ice rink. Fortunately, forecasters are calling for warmer temperatures, but they can't come soon enough.

Winter also has brought controversy. A resident of a nearby suburb called Critter

This ancient (by river otter standards) female, dubbed Miss Dame when she was rescued just before the turn of the year, is expected to spend the rest of her life at Critter Care because staff doubt she'll be able to fend for herself anymore. But that's okay. They'll make room for her.

Care to report a freezing orphaned bear cub huddled under his neighbour's picnic table. He called the Conservation Officer Service about the animal, too, but was told that no one could come until the next day, and when they did, they would simply chase it into the bushes. Critter Care told the resident not to handle the bear because it's unlawful for anyone other than a conservation officer (CO) or someone accredited

by the CO to touch bears. Instead, they suggested he call a sister organization called the Furbearers, which does have the appropriate accreditation and so were able to bring the bear to Langley.

But without knowing that, the Conservation Officer Service accused the resident of transporting the cub himself and threatened him with arrest and jail. It was only after media reported what actually happened that the service backed down and apologized.

Incidents like these put Critter Care in a difficult spot because, even though they believe the resident did the right thing, they have to be careful to follow government protocol or their licence to operate the refuge could be revoked. Not so Bryce Casavant, a former CO who was fired from the service for refusing to kill two bear cubs. He's free to tell it as it is, and his verdict is a harsh one. He says the hunting culture behind the Conservation Officer Service influences their behaviour and results in the kind of incident involving this cub. BC government statistics bear him out. In the eight years before this book was written, BC conservation officers killed more than 4,000 black bears, 160 grizzlies, and 780 cougars. That doesn't seem very much like "conservation."

A WEEK after he arrived, the cub, to everyone's surprise, is fine. Things looked grim for a while, says veterinary technician

This raccoon looks happy enough, but he won't be set free until spring. Critter Care never releases animals in winter, the most difficult season of the year for wildlife to find food.

Ciara O'Higgins, but he suddenly started eating and drinking and the worst was over. Now he's sharing a pen with Roxxy and is happy.

Meanwhile, a similar incident occurred with another cub and another CO. This time it was the officer who brought the cub to Critter Care, but he did it without protecting him from the weather. When the bear arrived at Critter Care, he was sedated in a wire pet carrier without blankets in the open bed of the officer's pickup. So thanks to the wind, the blowing snow, and the minus-double-digit temperature, when the cub arrived, he was shrouded in ice. He was so cold that he required round-the-clock care to get warm. But like the first cub, he survived and is doing well. Ciara says Critter Care asks COs repeatedly to wrap the animals they transport in blankets, but they can't force them to do so. Sometimes, Critter Care must deal with the consequences.

Mercifully, by the third weekend of the month the snow has become rain and the temperatures have crept above zero.

This deer mouse named Henry, then Henrietta on closer inspection, is proof that no animal is too small for Critter Care's attention. Actually all she needed was some warming up after being out in winter's chill too long.

The pipes are flowing again, a huge relief because now the enclosures can be cleaned properly and the animals' drinking water remains liquid instead of frozen solid.

The two cubs are better, too, but they still haven't been named. Ordinarily, staff or volunteers name Critter Care's animals, but only after seven days. First, they want to be sure the animal will survive, and second, they want time to get to know them. However, because of the media attention these cubs received, Critter Care is considering inviting the public to name them instead. In an online campaign before Christmas, supporters were asked to name six cubs who turned up in an unexpected pre-holiday blitz. Thus Ridge, Cinder, Decker, Hattie, Stormy, and Odin came to be. Now it's the snow cubs' turn.

MEANWHILE, OTHER animals have required attention, too. A deer mouse named Henry (renamed Henrietta upon closer inspection) has been returned to the wild after almost freezing to death. A squirrel with head trauma (and a bad attitude, says Nathan) is now living in the same backyard where he was rescued. And most miraculous of all, a skunk who hitched a 65-kilometre (40-mile) ride from Vancouver to the small community of Walnut Grove in the engine compartment of a Ford Mustang lived not only to see tomorrow, but also to spray her rescuers.

She was discovered by a team of startled car mechanics at an auto repair shop when the car's owner reported hearing odd noises coming from under the Mustang's hood. Amazingly, the skunk was unhurt, but she was also in no mood to leave. The engine compartment was warm and it was cold outside. At one point, she did climb on top of the engine, so Ciara suggested the mechanics build a ladder for her to climb down. They did, but the skunk still wouldn't budge. So it was finally left to Ciara and two interns to extricate her instead.

It took them half an hour to wrestle the adamant animal from the car. At one point, Ciara resorted to pulling her tail, which is when the skunk did what skunks always do when they're threatened. "Yes, we were quite fragrant when we got home," Ciara deadpans. The ungrateful skunk was released immediately.

With January over, staff are praying that it will be at least another month—maybe even two—before this year's orphaned infants begin to appear. But given how late they were being born last year, employees worry that they may arrive sooner. "No babies!" Nathan shouts defiantly. February and March will tell.

THERE TO THE END

GIVEN THE NATURE of what Critter Care does, it's inevitable that not every animal taken in will be made well. Unfortunately, some animals have to be euthanized. This month they included two raccoons and an opossum who turned out to be blind. It's not unusual for wild animals to go blind, says Ciara. They can develop cataracts—an opaque film over their eyes—just like people, especially when they grow old. In summer, when food is plentiful, they sometimes manage to get by using just their noses, but in winter, when everything is scarce, their health deteriorates quickly. Therefore, Critter Care had no choice but to put them down. When this happens, their bodies are cremated and their ashes are scattered on the society's grounds. That way they'll rest where their suffering ended.

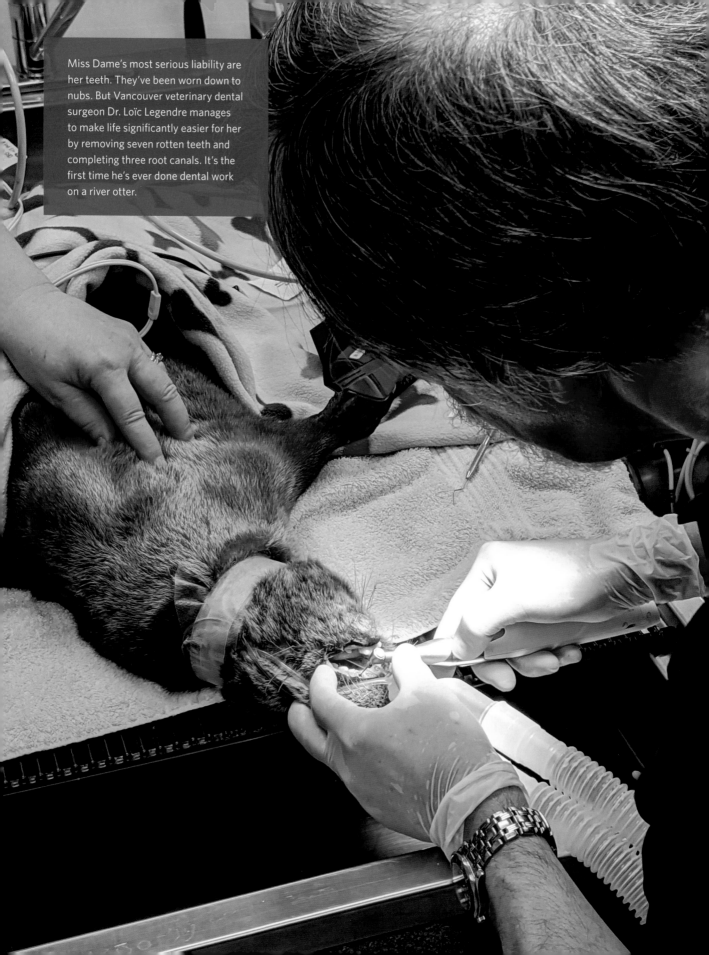

Miss Dame's most serious liability are her teeth. They've been worn down to nubs. But Vancouver veterinary dental surgeon Dr. Loïc Legendre manages to make life significantly easier for her by removing seven rotten teeth and completing three root canals. It's the first time he's ever done dental work on a river otter.

FEBRUARY

THE IDEA MAY seem outlandish, but then new ideas often do, and this is definitely something that hasn't been tried before. Nathan and a team of veterinary dental surgeons are going to meet this month to discuss the possibility of outfitting Dame Judi Dentures, Critter Care's ancient otter, with—you guessed it—dentures. Just like an over-eager hockey player's, only sharper. West Coast Veterinary Dental Services in Vancouver performs specialized dental work on all sorts of companion animals—dogs, cats, guinea pigs, ferrets, and rabbits. So, Nathan argues, why not a river otter?

As January's chapter explained, Dame's front teeth have been worn to nothing, meaning she can only eat mush and must never be released into the wild. But if dental surgeon Dr. Loïc Legendre can anchor a set of artificial canine teeth in Dame's mouth, she would be able to eat and catch the food river otters are supposed to eat—namely fish. It also would mean she would be the first river otter in history to be outfitted with dentures.

Even then, she won't be fit enough to live free, though Nathan hopes that with teeth she'll be able to act like a mother for orphaned otter pups who can be released back into the wild. He hopes she'll be able to teach them to swim *and* fish, skills essential in nature and something otters definitely need teeth for. And Dame might be around a long time to do that. In the wild, river

At the moment, Critter Care has 29 bears to look after. Everyone agrees this is far too many, but there is no alternative except to do their best. But the sooner some of those bears are released, the better.

otters are considered old if they live eight or nine years. But in captivity, they can live for 20. So if Dame is going to be with Critter Care that long, it would be nice if she had teeth.

Amazingly, a week later, it looks as if Nathan's idea could become real. He thought if Dame's surgery went ahead (and he wasn't sure it would), it would be months in the future. Instead, Dr. Legendre has scheduled it for a day usually dedicated to giving or receiving chocolate or flowers: Valentine's Day! Not only that, but her caregivers will find out if she's pregnant.

Female otters have a fantastic ability to delay getting pregnant after mating.

Depending on circumstances, a female otter can wait up to 10 months to conceive an embryo or not. Nature is her guide. If food is abundant, she'll probably conceive immediately. But if life is hard and there isn't as much to eat, she has up to ten months to "decide." Normally, otters bear two to four pups, and will spend a year looking after them before setting them free.

So it's possible that even though Dame shows no signs of being pregnant, she might be. An ultrasound will determine that before her surgery. Unfortunately, there's a risk that if she is pregnant, her pups may not survive because of the surgeon's anaesthetic. But Nathan believes

To ease the bear burden, Critter Care is having another bear pen built. When it's finished, it will look like this one. But bad weather keeps holding up its construction.

that's a risk they have to take because Dame really can't live without teeth. The only certainty is that, whatever happens, it will be a big day for her.

When that day finally arrives, however, things don't go quite as planned. Upon meeting Dame, dentist to otter, Dr. Legendre realizes it will take three visits, not one, to implant her dentures, and each visit will require her to be anaesthetized. That's too dangerous for an otter Dame's age, says Nathan, so Dr. Legendre limits himself to extracting seven rotten teeth and performing three root canals. It's a first for him. He has performed root canals on a sea otter, polar bear, lion,

cheetah, wolverine, and elephant, but never a river otter.

The procedure means Dame will be able to eat actual fish now instead of fish mush. But with her worn teeth, she still won't be able to catch them, so Critter Care's orphaned pups will have to learn that critical skill from someone else. Dame can still teach them to swim, though, as well as how to respond to other otters and to mark their territories. And no, she's not pregnant. A blessing or a sorrow? That's only for her to know.

OF COURSE, Critter Care staff have more on their minds than just Dame's teeth.

The two bear cubs who were brought to Critter Care in January almost frozen to death have made a quick and complete recovery. They're now known as Frosty and Rocky.

With so many bears to look after—29 after the arrival of January's cubs—the refuge has commissioned a fourth bear enclosure. Even with discounts from the builders and suppliers, the cost is around $100,000. It's a colossal sum, but the enclosure is essential. Staff hoped it would be finished before the end of the month, but bad weather keeps interfering (it snowed again on February 4), so the enclosure is still a steel skeleton. At this point, there's no telling when it will be complete. All anyone can say is the sooner, the better.

February is also mating season for raccoons, skunks, coyotes, otters, beavers, and other animals. In many animal species,

fathers rarely stick around to help raise their young, so choosing a mate is always left to the mother. What she wants is someone strong and healthy who will pass on a promising set of genes to her offspring. Unlike the elaborate rituals of human courtship, there's nothing romantic about it. No one delivers champagne and flowers in the forest. One of the best ways male mammals demonstrate their vigour is by fighting and beating each other, which can, and often does, result in injuries— injuries Critter Care ends up treating.

Bears and deer have similarly business-like nuptials, but theirs occur months later. Both bears and deer have long gestation

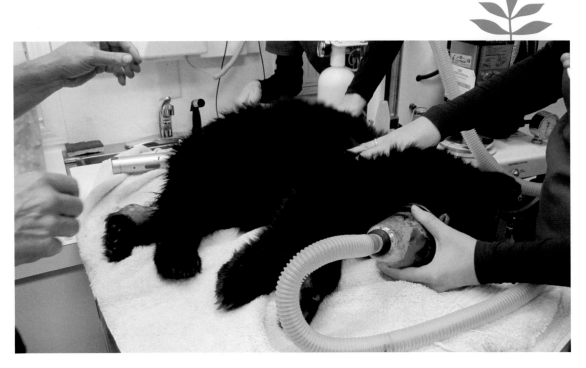

Critter Care does everything it can to cure the sick and heal the injured, including engaging top-flight veterinary surgeons to work on particularly difficult cases. Here, Dr. Ken Macquisten works on the paw of a bear cub.

periods: For black bears, it's 220 days, and for black-tailed deer, southern BC's most common deer species, it's 203. As a result, bears mate in summer and deer in early fall. However, that's where the similarity ends. Bears give birth in winter while they are cocooned in warm dens dug under downy quilts of insulating snow. Mothers-to-be will enter their dens in December, but they won't give birth until January. Then they remain in the dens until March while the cubs nurse and grow. What's extraordinary about this is that, for the most part, the mother bear will be asleep while it happens. Of course, she wakes up to give birth, but then, in very short order,

she turns over and goes back to sleep again. The cubs attach themselves to her to suckle her while she's fast asleep.

By contrast, deer remain outside in the cold all winter, still pregnant, and still trying to feed themselves and their growing young during what is undoubtedly the toughest time of the year. The only way they manage is by moving continually and searching everywhere they can for food. Traditionally, deer give birth in May or June, but given the way the seasons are changing as a result of climate change, those births could come earlier in future. Who's to say? All Critter Care can do is look after them if and when they arrive.

One of February's most dramatic events involved a skunk like this one getting caught up in traffic on one of Vancouver's busiest bridges. The skunk was rescued, but sadly had to be put down because of a broken leg.

fun stuff for the bears' amusement: logs, hammocks, climbing apparatuses, tunnels, and pools. O'Higgins hopes it'll be done by March. Fingers crossed!

February ends with the naming, at last, of the two bear cubs that were rescued in January. The cub who was saved by the man whose kindness earned him threats of imprisonment has been called Rocky after Rocky Mountaineer, a company specialising in train travel and a long-time donor to Critter Care that paid the costs of Rocky's recovery. The other bear has been named Frosty in recognition of the semi-frozen state he was in when he arrived. In the end, both names were chosen by Critter Care staff when it occurred to them that inviting the public to select the names might rekindle tensions between the sanctuary and conservation officers— something they'd rather avoid.

And there are still no orphaned babies, but March is only a calendar page away.

AS THE month progresses, the building of the bear enclosure has moved apace, thanks to a welcome stretch of sunshine. The roof is up, and the concrete floor is solid. Now all that's left to do is construct some wooden dens—Critter Care employs two full-time handymen—and install some

TRAFFIC NIGHTMARE

IN MID-MONTH, A bizarre incident that should have had a happy ending didn't. Somehow a young skunk found himself dodging traffic on one of the main bridges leading out of Vancouver. Thousands of cars use this bridge daily, but one morning, there among the roaring motors, was a skunk. Who knows how or why he got there? The important thing was to get him off the bridge. To facilitate this, an officer with the Royal Canadian Mounted Police went so far as to stop traffic on the bridge while a brave Critter Care volunteer trapped the animal. (Of course she got sprayed for her trouble.) But alas, the skunk didn't make it. His leg was broken, so he had to be put down. People recover from broken legs all the time, but animals—especially wild animals—aren't that lucky. They can't cope with having their legs plastered for six weeks while they heal, so Critter Care sometimes has to make the difficult decision to euthanize them instead.

Veterinary technician Nathan Wagstaffe, Critter Care's otter expert, is the first to hold the pups from this surprising litter.

MARCH

I T'S HAPPENED. The first babies have arrived. Two black squirrels, a brother and sister, two weeks old and no bigger than a pair of iPhones, were deposited at Critter Care on March 10. They were born in a nest atop a house in a nearby suburb. The house was being reroofed and their nest was destroyed. As a result, the mother ran off, leaving her two blind kits behind. Now, they're curled up in a green woollen hat nestled in a tumble of colourful baby blankets in a clear plastic tub in the society's nursery. Nathan reckons they'll need two months of care.

There are a number of reasons why wildlife babies can become orphaned, but two of those have to do with people. Sometimes it happens accidentally. A mother skunk may root through someone's garbage for food and trap her head in a plastic cup. Without anyone to free her, she'll suffocate and die, leaving her kits alone. Other times, the harm is inflicted deliberately. Some people view urban wildlife as pests, so it's not uncommon, for example, for them to poison, trap, or even shoot mice, raccoons, skunks, coyotes, and other animals to get rid of them.

Whatever the circumstance, it happens regularly. The squirrel pair are merely the first of what could be a tidal wave of foundlings. Last year, Critter Care raised more than 1,500 orphaned baby animals. In June alone, the busiest month of the year, they

▲ This beaver was discovered with a growth on one of his hind legs that turned out to be cancerous. Sadly, that meant he had to be put down, leaving his family without a father. Beavers are rarities in the animal world in that males play an active role in the rearing of their young.

➤ This skunk had her head stuck in a can. She would have suffocated if someone hadn't removed it.

had 500. That's why every person at Critter Care, from regular staff to interns and volunteers, are so essential. How else would they cope with numbers that large?

While Critter Care had expected the squirrels, they're surprised—and troubled—by the number of raccoons that have come through the society's gates suffering from distemper, a contagious viral disease. In just over a week, Wagstaffe has seen 10. During the whole of last year, there were only four. Skunks

are also getting sick, but lab tests haven't revealed why. Whatever the reason, it's worrying.

And, it turns out, temporary. In just a few days, the flow of animals brought in to the society has stopped. To everyone's relief, it ended as abruptly as it began. No one knows why. Nature is full of mysteries. This is another.

LATER IN MARCH, there is some good news. Dame, the otter, is swimming again.

She's even catching fish. Only slow-moving goldfish, but that's still something. For her, it's a rebirth.

Not only that, a week after they arrived, the squirrels—who are doing splendidly—are starting to look like a false alarm. No more babies have followed them. The staff are relieved because last year the first babies didn't arrive until March 28, so they feared this year might bring an early onslaught. Not so far. A good omen? We'll see.

Meanwhile, older animals continue to get into trouble that Critter Care has to get them out of. It took three days of trying, but eventually Nathan managed to net a beaver with a growth on his hind leg. It could be an abscess that can be treated, or a tumour that can't. A biopsy will determine the answer.

Although staff are accustomed to having to put animals down (a sad reality of the job), beavers are different because unlike most other wildlife, they lead close family lives. If it turns out this beaver does have cancer and has to be euthanized, his death will be a blow to whatever family he enjoys. If he has a mate, it's possible she may be pregnant. Beavers usually mate for life, and when they have kits, the babies remain with them for two years even though the female beaver will likely bear more kits

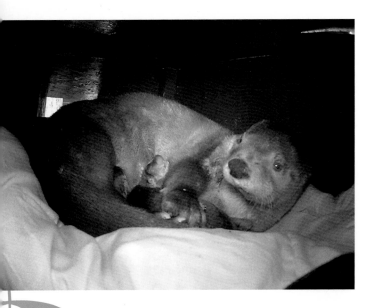

Miss Dame astonished everyone at Critter Care when she gave birth to three pups this month, two boys and a girl. No one even knew she was pregnant.

the following spring. Consequently, beaver lodges can get crowded rather quickly. While mothers nurse their young, fathers maintain the lodge they live in and gather food for the whole family.

But doting as beaver parents are, when a kit is two years old, it's time for them to leave the lodge and begin life anew. However, with the wilderness constantly shrinking as humans take over more and more of it, that's often easier said than done. So it isn't unusual for Critter Care to rescue nomadic two-year-olds from places they shouldn't be—such as people's gardens—and relocate them to areas where a start is still possible. They will even build temporary lodges for them: just wood huts festooned with branches,

but lifesavers for the beavers until they're prepared to build lodges of their own.

Regrettably, the male beaver's biopsy confirms the worst. The growth on his leg is cancerous, so staff have no choice but to euthanize him. Of course, we'll never know the fate of his mate, if he had one, but Nathan reckons that if he did, she'll eventually find a new partner. Animals do grieve, but they're also practical.

A second beaver is luckier. He was found breathing queerly by a passerby in Stanley Park, Vancouver's largest and most famous park. But all he has is a sinus infection. He's also about two years old, so when he's released it will be somewhere new where he can hopefully have a fresh start.

There is also more good news about Dame. In fact, it's not just good, it's astounding. She has given birth to three pups! Yes, an ultrasound in February declared she wasn't pregnant, but either someone made a mistake or the pups were too small to be detected. Whatever the truth, a volunteer who went to clean her den on March 22 found her with two newborns. Five hours later there was a third: a female and two males. "We were amazed," says Nathan. That's putting it mildly. Unfortunately, this also means Dame will be too busy raising her own pups to bother with others, but never mind—no one's going to carp at a miracle. It's the first otter birth in Critter Care history.

Here they are, living proof of Miss Dame's astounding parlour trick: Custard, Jam, and Scone, named in honour of the aristocratic English custom of high tea.

TWO DAYS LATER, a less momentous, but equally welcome, blessing arrives: the new bear enclosure is finished. It's going be home to eight of Critter Care's twenty-nine bears, including Roxxy and Rocky, who were rescued in late December and mid-January, respectively. They were tiny then but have been eating like, well, bears ever since, and have grown accordingly. The biggest of the eight is about the size of a German shepherd, only *much* heavier. Roxxy and Rocky aren't nearly as large, but they needn't be afraid of bigger inmates. Bear cubs, regardless of size, almost always get along because they're used to having siblings, so eight living side-by-side shouldn't be a problem.

As well, two more squirrel babies have arrived. They fell out of a chimney. Sadly, one was too badly hurt to recover, but his sister is improving slowly. But that's it in terms of orphans. The storm is still gathering.

BY THE END of March, it still hasn't hit, but spring is when babies are born, and there's never been a year when some of those babies weren't orphaned.

This yellow-bellied marmot hitched a ride in a car's engine compartment all the way from Kamloops, a city about 350 kilometres (215 miles) away from Langley. But other than being displaced, there's nothing wrong with him. So Wagstaffe has volunteered to drive him home.

Dame, however, is looking after her pups single-handedly. Week-old otter pups don't do much more than nurse, sleep, and expel waste, but they need help with that. This means otter mums, like many animal mothers, have to lick their offspring to stimulate them to pee and poo. It's probably safe to assume human mothers are relieved not to be among them.

The pups also have names: Custard, Jam, and Scone. Have you ever heard of English high tea? For years aristocratic English families took tea at 4 o'clock when, in addition to their fine porcelain cups of Assam or Lapsang Souchong, they would enjoy plates of scones with jam and custard, among other delectables. So, with Dame being a Dame, the names seemed appropriate.

The society also has an out-of-town guest: a yellow-bellied marmot who hitched a ride in a car's engine compartment from Kamloops, about 350 kilometres (215 miles) northeast of Vancouver. Why? Because Kamloops was cold and the engine compartment was warm. The trouble is that the marmot is now a very long way away from home. Nathan will drive him back sometime next month.

Traditionally, April marks the official start of baby season. Will this year be the exception that tests that rule? It's unlikely, but only time will tell. Regardless, staff are bracing themselves.

A HECK OF A MESS

SOMETHING STAFF AND interns never get a break from is cleaning. Take bears. Twenty-nine create a tremendous amount of mess that has to be cleaned continually. How much mess? Twenty-nine bears eat two tonnes of food a day. That's right, two *tonnes*.

Fruit, vegetables, fish, eggs, even kibble. Almost all of it is donated by supermarkets or individuals who grow food in their gardens or catch one too many fish. And with all that food going in, imagine how much dung comes out.

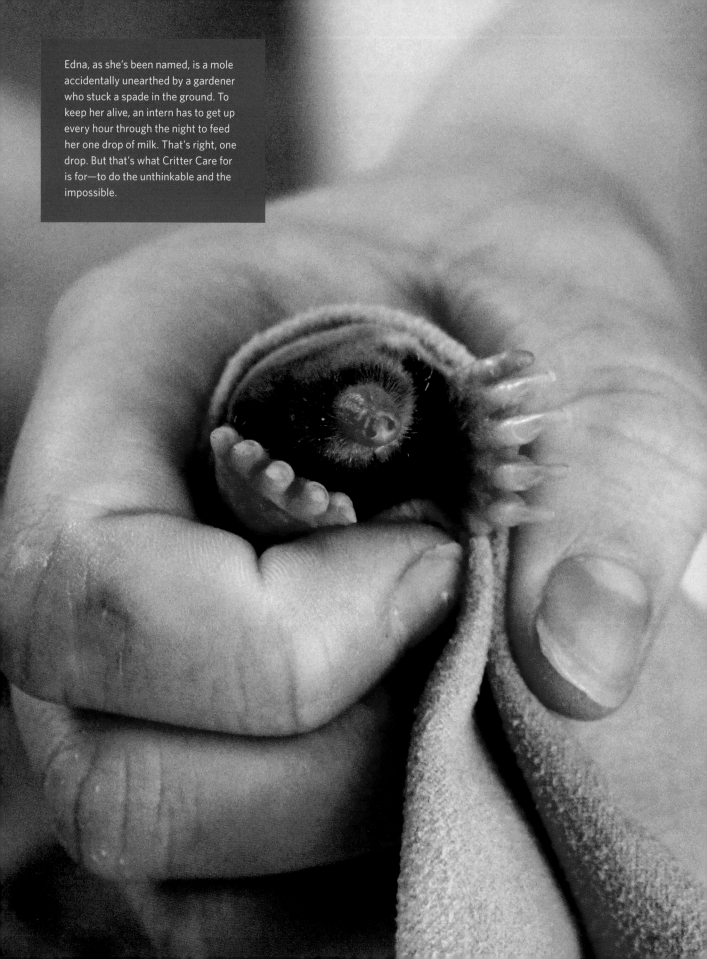

Edna, as she's been named, is a mole accidentally unearthed by a gardener who stuck a spade in the ground. To keep her alive, an intern has to get up every hour through the night to feed her one drop of milk. That's right, one drop. But that's what Critter Care for is for—to do the unthinkable and the impossible.

APRIL

S SOON AS April arrives, babies do too, as if on cue. Seven squirrels, five rabbits, and a mole. The mole has muted grey, velvety fur, is about as big (or small) as your thumb, and is as demanding as a duchess. She and two siblings were uncovered when a gardener stuck a spade in the ground. The gardener didn't mean to unearth them, but when she did, she called Critter Care. Sadly, the siblings failed to endure the upheaval. Baby moles need to be fed every hour, twenty-four hours a day, and the unfortunate pair missed too many feedings to survive, although the one who did is fine. To keep her that way, however, a heroic intern has to get up every hour through the night to feed her a drop of milk. Literally one drop.

Sally Brad, a 20-year-old student of animal conservation science at the University of Cumbria in England, is one of the "lucky" caregivers tasked with doing this. And she loves it. "She's beautiful and so sweet," Sally says of Edna, as the mole's been named. "You wake her up and she yawns and then she gets all wriggly."

Equally amazing is that Sally isn't a zombie the next day. "I thought I would be, but I'm okay. Somehow I manage to stay awake."

Thanks to Sally, within a week, Edna is growing and slowly turning black, the colour of adult moles.

Because rabbits breed like, well, rabbits, rabbit babies are always arriving at Critter Care needing help. Who could resist these two?

Squirrels and bunnies also have to be fed frequently and regularly, but mercifully not at night. They are fed using syringes with nipples fixed to the tips. The bunnies drink commercial cat milk (or a similar formula), while the squirrels receive a liquid concocted by a company in Arizona that synthesizes milk formulas for almost every kind of North American wild mammal. Raccoon, mink, skunk, fawn—you name it and they have it. Except rabbit, for some reason, which is why the bunnies

drink kitten milk. In a busy year, Critter Care can spend around $90,000 on the stuff.

Baby animals also have to be burped. Raccoons are often draped over the carer's shoulder like a human baby, but rabbits and squirrels are happy to be laid in the palm of the carer's hand and have their backs tapped gently. Any time a mammal baby—human or otherwise—drinks formula, he or she must be burped. Because of this, when things get busy later in the year, you'll find the Critter Care nursery floor crowded with patient interns burping gaseous babies.

How much care each animal receives depends on the kind of animal it is. Rabbits and moles can leave after a month. Squirrels need two. Raccoons, up to 10. But whatever the species, one thing is certain: the moment one leaves, another will be along soon to take its place.

THE SECOND WEEK of April belongs mainly to raccoons. Four babies arrive (along with more squirrels, bunnies, another deer mouse, and another mole) and 25 almost-adults are released. The babies, who are about a week old, are adopted by Critter Care vice-president Lynda Brown, who will care for them for a month. Baby raccoons require a lot of attention, so Lynda is literally going to be their surrogate mother. She'll nurse them 10 times a day, amuse them with toys (toilet rolls filled with herbs, small stuffed animals, and things from nature such as leaves, twigs, and nuts), and "stimulate" them to pee and poo by rubbing their genitals with tissue. You might remember that Dame, the otter, does this with her tongue. Once the month is up and the raccoons seem ready, they'll return to the refuge.

During their time at Critter Care, raccoons learn how to forage for food, socialize with other raccoons, and build a

Sometimes distressed animals are flown in by helicopter. That's right, helicopter. It's much better than battling traffic.

den. They live in small groups (siblings are always kept together) and are released in groups, too. That way they can either stay together or go their own way.

But all that's months away. For some raccoons it may not come until next spring. Meantime, Lynda's raccoons—two males and two females—are beginning their lives in a clear plastic incubator in her dining room, with a Teddy bear for company and a jumble of soft bedding to sleep in. They're so young that their eyes and ears are still

▲ Former commercial pilot Norm Snihur wanted something useful to do after he retired. He found that something when he signed up to volunteer at a wild bird sanctuary. Now he flies all over southern BC rescuing wild animals and delivering them to rehabilitation centres like Critter Care.

➤ Miss Dame's otter babies, Custard, Jam, and Scone, are growing, but they're a lot for an otter of Miss Dame's age to handle. So Scone, the female, is going to leave her mother and join the society's orphaned pups.

clamped shut. All they do is eat and sleep in a snuggly cluster of each other's fur. Each is about the size of a small yam.

At this age, they are completely dependent on Lynda, who feeds them every two and a half hours during the day and at 12:30 and 4:30 AM at night. The process takes about an hour, as each raccoon is fed individually, burped, and made to pee and poo twice, both before and after nursing. But like Sally, Lynda loves it. After all her years as a volunteer, she knows that one day, because of her efforts, these raccoons will be free, too. She's had the privilege of enjoying that special moment many times in her career, and it never gets old.

BEFORE THE BABY raccoons are ready for release, however, it's the bears' turn. Eight are due to be sprung this month. Ordinarily, Critter Care would never release bears before July, when the province's annual spring bear hunt ends. But 29 bears are simply too many to cope with, and these eight are definitely ready to go. Because the British Columbia government considers bears to be dangerous, freeing them is the responsibility of conservation officers. The last Critter Care gets to see of them is when they're loaded into special barrel-like carriers in the beds of government pickup trucks that will deliver them to freedom.

"It's hard," says Nathan. "We put a full year into them and then we have to say good-bye to them as they drive off."

What makes it doubly hard is that the reason Critter Care has so many bears are the very conservation officers charged with releasing them. A year ago, news reports were full of stories about COs shooting allegedly troublesome mothers and then carting their suddenly orphaned cubs off to Langley. The public was not happy, so this year COs promised to intervene earlier and relocate more. Let's hope that results in some positive change.

In the meantime, there is still more news about Dame. Unfortunately, given her age, she's unable to produce enough milk for three hungry pups, so one of them— Scone, her daughter—has been adopted by

Nathan in the same way Lynda adopted her raccoons. A smart move. This way, all three pups will have a better chance at survival. When Scone finishes nursing, she'll return to her mother. Because if your aim is to live as an otter, your best teacher is another otter.

As it happens, April's waning days bring yet another one. However, this one has the distinction of arriving via helicopter, flown by an 81-year-old retired airline pilot named Norm Snihur, who uses his private chopper to collect distressed wildlife from all over southern Vancouver Island and southwestern BC. Norm, who now lives in Nanaimo, began rescuing animals in 1994, after he started volunteering for a suburban Vancouver rehabilitation centre that cared for raptors. Since then, he's recovered more than 1,700 animals—birds and mammals—many of whom came to Critter Care. He makes about four or five deliveries to the society each year.

The curious thing about Norm is that until he started working at the raptor sanctuary, he had no particular fondness for animals. He decided to volunteer there because he thought it might be interesting. It was only when he realized what a service he could perform as a pilot that his life changed. Even now, he's remarkably modest. Ask him about his life-saving derring-do and he replies: "It gives me something worthwhile to do."

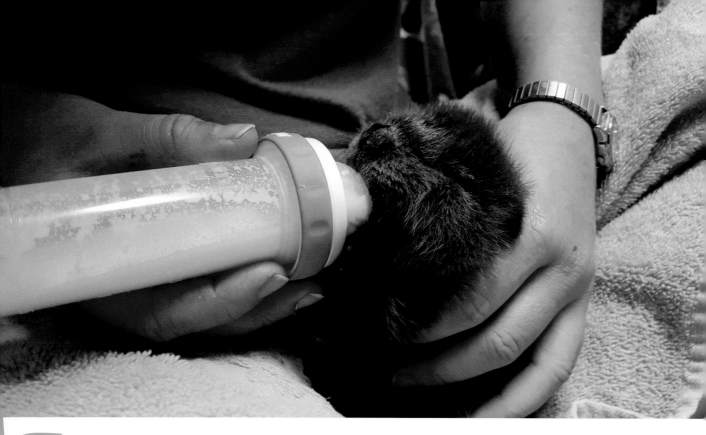

Critter Care spends tens of thousands of dollars every year buying formula from a US company that manufactures formula specially tailored for animals of almost every kind—like this beaver.

Meanwhile, baby season continues to live up to its name with the arrival of still more raccoons, rabbits, and a marmot. The rabbits are predominantly eastern cottontails—tawny brown creatures with dark speckles on their backs. As adults, they're about as big as a man's running shoe—with ears—but as Critter Care orphans, they're more the size of ping pong balls. Eastern cottontail rabbits live almost everywhere in the US and southern Canada and breed, well, like rabbits. A female cottontail can have up to seven litters in a year, but mostly have four or five. The admittedly harsh reason for this is that so many other species eat them. Coyotes, owls, eagles, hawks, raccoons, bobcats, and even otters. In fact, rabbits are so widely preyed upon that they're sometimes known—not very kindly—as "nature's granola."

A RARE VISITOR

AS YOU KNOW by now, Critter Care's primary patients are bears, skunks, raccoons, squirrels, and rabbits. But April brings a fairly rare resident: a dark brown snowshoe hare. Yes, such hares do turn white in winter to blend in with their snowy surroundings, but they owe their name not to the white stuff, but to their large, snowshoe-like hind feet that prevent them from sinking into snow drifts when they run and hop.

In just six days, Critter Care has received 67 new animals, almost all of them orphaned babies, including this tiny bunny.

MAY

THE ARRIVAL OF May marks the departure of Edna. The once teeny mole is now big enough (picture a sausage) to survive on her own. But first, staff want to make certain she'll be properly prepared. So, in the spot where she'll be released, they use a spade and some toilet roll tubes to construct a system of underground tunnels that she can move into straight away. This is typical of how Critter Care likes to ensure that its clients get the best possible start, since parting is such sweet sorrow.

However, Edna's leaving is the exception, not the rule. In just six days, the society receives 67 new animals, mostly baby raccoons, squirrels, and rabbits. Ciara is surprised because May is usually when opossums, skunks, and fawns start to appear, too. But so far, they've seen nary a one. No one knows why.

They did get an urgent call about an abandoned fawn, however, from a man who insisted she be rescued immediately. He was mistaken, though. Mother deer often leave their young for up to twelve hours while they forage for food. Meanwhile, the fawns, who are well hidden, curl up quietly and await their mother's return. What's so remarkable about this is that baby deer have evolved so they don't emit a scent that could attract predators. Nary a whiff. Critter Care always suggests callers wait a day before disturbing babies to make sure their mothers come back to

May usually brings an onslaught of baby opossums, skunks, and fawns. This year, it was delayed for some reason. But when it came, it came. This newborn opossum was part of it.

them, which is what happened in this case. Because babies are always better off with their mums.

Not that Critter Care won't go (literally) to great lengths to rescue animals who genuinely need saving. Genelle is a tiny community about a seven-hour drive away from Critter Care. It was also, until this week, the home of a distressed Columbian ground squirrel rescued by an elderly couple whose neighbour wanted it gone by any means possible. You may never have heard of a Columbian ground squirrel, but they're about the size of a tennis ball can, have brown, black, or grey fur, and live throughout the Pacific Northwest.

This particular squirrel in Genelle had trouble keeping upright, so the couple wanted Critter Care to look after her. Easier said than done. Because Critter Care

May has also brought its share of skunks, who have a nasty habit of not knowing when they should be grateful. Even when you help one, you can pretty well count on being blasted. Skunks only have to be two hours old to know how to shoot.

doesn't have a dedicated transport service, it often has to rely on volunteers, so in this case the delivery took two days, two vehicles, and three teams of caregivers. But now the squirrel, who's been named Dandy, is in Langley, on antibiotics and feeling better.

With time, she's also rounder and starting to dig the dirt inside her pen. Both these observations may mean nothing, or they may suggest she's pregnant. By digging the dirt, is she really digging a den? Ciara has made arrangements to get her back to Genelle by the middle of the month, unless she gives birth first. *If* she gives birth. In that case, she and her young (she could have up to seven) will have to remain in Langley for four more weeks until the kits are weaned. No one wants this. All wild animals are better

This young male coyote orphan travelled all the way from the BC–Alberta border to get to Critter Care. He made the trip courtesy of a long-haul trucker, one of a network of them in the province who transport helpless animals to and from places they need to be.

But, as anyone who's been around illness knows, it can be unpredictable as well as unforgiving.

EVEN FARTHER away than Genelle is the town of Golden, near the BC–Alberta border. That's where a young coyote began his journey to Critter Care, courtesy of a long-haul trucker who made room for him in his rig. He is Critter Care's first coyote of the year. It turns out that Wayne, the driver (Ciara didn't catch his surname), is part of a community of truckers in the southeastern part of the province who carry shelter animals to and from places they need to be. Further proof that generosity knows no bounds.

After the obligatory seven days of observation have passed, Ciara decides to name the coyote Lucifer, not because there's anything devilish about him, but because she's a fan of the Netflix series. And happily, he's doing well, though he's proved to be a fussy eater. Give him beef, and he'll lap it up heartily. Give him lamb, and he'll sniff in disgust.

Critter Care welcomed 86 new animals in the week Dandy arrived (mainly baby raccoons, rabbits, and squirrels), but it also saw the departure of three more bears and three otters. Good thing, too, because when it comes to bears and otters, the society's seams are splitting. Before the otters left, Critter Care had nine, a record.

off giving birth in the wild, but with no way to get Dandy back to Genelle before the weekend, all anyone can do is wait, hope, and pray.

Sadly, in the end all such worries prove not to matter. On the same weekend Ciara had planned to take her home, Dandy suddenly became gravely ill. With what, no one knew. Staff did their best for her, but in the end she had to be euthanized. No one expected this. Dandy had been fine.

The ninth, a baby female, flew in on Norm Snihur's helicopter not long after his first otter delivery last month. Now six remain: Dame and her three pups, Jam, Custard, and Scone; two unrelated female pups named Bubble and Squeak; and the pup who arrived by helicopter. All of them are still nursing, the males by Dame, and the females by Nathan. No one knows how things will work once they're weaned. Will Dame accept Bubble and Squeak? Will she welcome Scone back? Fortunately, there are still a few weeks before the pups are weaned, but it's better to be prepared in case things go sideways.

Another week finally brings the expected, but mysteriously delayed, onslaught of baby skunks, opossums, and fawns. It means, says Ciara, that baby season has officially begun. Babies are kept in one of two facilities: the nursery, or the cozily named "small mammal hotel." The nursery is brimming with raccoons. When you first enter, you don't realize how many there are because they're so small—the size of a squirrel minus the tail—and because they're kept in large plastic incubator-like containers. But when you look closer, you realize that they're there, and there, and there, too.

Appropriately, the room is cheerful in the way that children's daycares are. There are bright colours and soft surfaces everywhere. There are also stuffed toys

Holmes is the first of Critter Care's annual crop of motherless fawns, meaning he has the whole fawn enclosure to himself at the moment. But that's not expected to last.

and kindly interns who feed the raccoons, comfort them, burp them, and attend to all their needs.

Last week, Critter Care had two newborn fawns to care for; this week it has one. Holmes, as he's been named, lost his mother and was found being attacked by a pair of adult deer who, because he wasn't theirs, wanted nothing to do with him. So he definitely needed saving. But the other fawn was rescued by a group of construction workers from the site where they were working. They said she was alone and

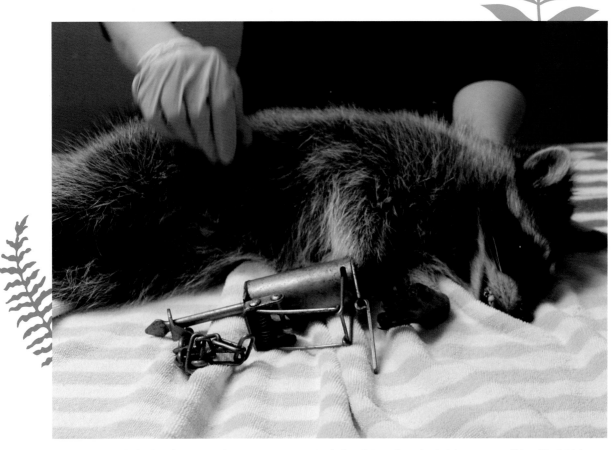

Despite years of pleading from animal-protection groups, including Critter Care, leghold traps are still legal in British Columbia. Animals who are caught in them suffer horrible agonies that sometimes leave Critter Choice no choice but to euthanize them.

suffering, but at Critter Care she seemed fine. She wasn't even hungry. So staff immediately began to suspect she was the victim of good intentions gone awry. She was. The workers phoned a few hours later to say a doe had been spotted on the site and the fawn was probably hers. Mother and baby were reunited quickly.

So Holmes is now living alone in the society's fawn enclosure, a grassy area with lots of trees about the size of a city backyard. It's an awfully big place for one small fawn, but Ciara says there have been years when Critter Care has had more than 20, so they have to be ready. After all, baby season is still in full tilt.

Month's end also brings some particularly disturbing news. An adult raccoon and skunk were found caught in leghold traps, infamous for locking their prey in agonizing vice-like grips. Sometimes the animal is so desperate to escape, he'll chew his leg off. The raccoon couldn't be saved; she had to be euthanized immediately. The skunk was luckier. She suffered no broken bones and was able to be released.

Theoretically, there's a law against placing leghold traps in urban or suburban areas, but it's flouted all the time. Anyone can buy a leghold trap online, and they're very easy to hide, so it's difficult to enforce the law. Proof is the increasing number of leghold trap victims whom Critter Care cares for each year. Last year saw 27, a record.

Animal-protection groups have been asking governments for years to ban leghold traps because they are so unreservedly cruel, but they've never succeeded. It's unfortunate, but BC has always been a place where people who love animals find themselves continually having to fight battles to save them...battles they rarely win.

A STING IN THEIR TAILS

JUST LIKE HUMAN babies, baby animals can and do get angry or upset sometimes. Usually, this happens when they're frightened. Some of them will squeal or bark, while others, like bunnies, do nothing at all. However, baby skunks really do have a sting in—actually just below—their tails. They're able to trigger their gag-inducing repellent at just a couple weeks old, meaning anyone looking after them can count on being blasted. Fortunately, baby skunk repellent isn't nearly as malodorous as the adult version. It takes only one or two washes to get the stench out of your clothes. If you're sprayed by an adult, it can take 10.

June has brought more orphaned fawns to Critter Care. Here an intern feeds one with some specially prepared fawn formula.

JUNE

J UNE BEGINS WITH a shocking revelation involving twin fawns, a company that trains animals for films and TV, and, the BC Conservation Officer Service.

This story actually started in the middle of May. Critter Care received a call from a bird sanctuary about 90 kilometres (55 miles) north of Langley about a pair of orphaned fawns who had been spotted in the area. Critter Care said it would accept them if someone could capture them, but then heard nothing more about them. Until the beginning of June, that is, when they learned that, with the permission of the BC Ministry of Environment, a for-profit business called Beyond Bears had "rescued" the fawns with the intention of raising and training them for the entertainment industry.

Fortunately, the story was reported by an online news service. Otherwise Critter Care and other animal-protection groups would never have known about it. When they did find out, their outrage was explosive. The subsequent public outcry meant the government couldn't ignore it. While the ministry did not admit any wrongdoing, it did reverse course by ordering a pair of COs to transfer the fawns to Critter Care. They arrived sick and badly bloated with severe diarrhea.

Additionally, early June brings an unwelcome milestone: On June 8, Critter Care receives its thousandth animal of the year.

With so many raccoons to look after, Critter Care has to do its best to keep them amused. This one is happy with a children's toy for the moment, but who knows how long that will last?

On the same date a year ago, it had 785. One of the main reasons for this increase is likely the shrinking wilderness as humans continue to encroach into wildlife habitats. As a result, there are more and more conflicts between humans and wildlife that almost always leave wildlife on the losing side. In fact, a quarter of all the raccoon babies currently at Critter Care were brought there by exterminators. A provincial law forbids disturbing a raccoon nest while the kits are 12 weeks or younger, even if the nest is in someone's dwelling.

But that doesn't mean people obey it. Critter Care's over-crowded nursery is proof of this.

With the facilities so full and busy, staff are also proposing to say good-bye to their last 18 bears, including Roxxy, Rocky, and Frosty, the cubs rescued in winter. Critter Care usually lets its bears go after July 1, when BC's spring bear hunt ends. But with so many bears to wrangle at once, they want to speed things up this year. To help make this possible, the government has agreed to release the bears in areas where

It's time to let the last of Critter Care's bears go. That means tranquilizing them so they can be loaded onto a truck that will take them back to the forest. Here Drs. Ken Macquisten and Louise Allmark size up the task at hand.

hunting is forbidden, so they may hit the road in as little as 10 days. Whatever happens, everyone hopes that once they're gone, Critter Care will be cub-free for a while. Because after 29, everyone needs a break.

THEY MAY need one, but that doesn't mean they're going to get one. In the middle of the month, a CO delivers two tiny cubs, a male and female, to Critter Care founder and resident mama bear Gail Martin, who often looks after newly arrived cubs. While she's at work, they will join her in her office, and when she goes home, they go home with her, too.

In addition to the cubs, two more fawns have arrived, bringing the total to five (a second male arrived soon after Holmes last month). There are also more otter pups. Again, it's anyone's guess how Dame and all these youngsters will get along when and if they have to.

June 30, the last day of the month and thankfully the last day of BC's bear hunt, is also the day when the society's

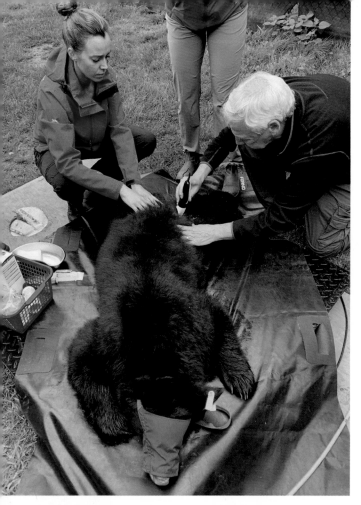

last releasable bears, Roxxy, Cinnamon, and Melon, will be let go. The latter half of June has already seen the release of 15 other bears at different times on different days. The bears' releases have had to be staggered because of all the work that goes into releasing them. Consequently, only so many can go at the same time. And now, at last, it's Roxxy's, Cinnamon's, and Melon's turn.

Essentially, the mission is this: Moving a half-grown bear (some weighing 90 kilograms, or 200 pounds, or more) into the back of a pickup truck that will take them to the wilderness and freedom. Easy peasy, right? Maybe if it were your neighbour's dog being transferred. But remember, these are bears, not beagles. Wild creatures with big teeth and sharp claws. So there's nothing easy about it.

First, two veterinarians, Dr. Ken Macquisten and Dr. Louise Allmark, have to sedate each bear with a dart. That means going into the bears' enclosure with a tranquilizer rifle and shooting each animal—slowly, one at a time, and in a spot with lots of muscle tissue, such as their thighs—with tranquilizer fluid. The difficulty depends on the bear. Most require one shot, but poor Roxxy, who zigzags back and forth like a pinball, requires several. The dart injects the bears with a sedative that puts them each to sleep. Then it's usually safe to carry each of the massive creatures, big teeth and sharp claws and

◄ After tranquilizing a bear, Drs. Macquisten and Allmark will weigh him or her and take a blood sample before waking him or her up again.

◄ When a bear is tranquilized, it's the last opportunity Critter Care staff have to say good-bye to an animal they have spent months looking after. It can be a bittersweet moment, to say the least.

▲ Using just their own strength, staff and volunteers pick up this tranquilized bear and prepare to move him or her into a Conservation Officer Service bear drum. Once the bear is safely inside, Drs. Macquisten and Allmark will inject him or her with a serum that will undo the effects of the sedative they administered earlier.

all, to a scale outside, where they will be weighed and samples of their blood and DNA will be taken. (Staff also like to use this opportunity, their last and safest, to pose for pictures with each bear.)

The next step involves placing the sleeping bruin inside a strong steel kennel—like a dog kennel, only larger and sturdier—where Dr. Allmark and Dr. Macquisten will inject each bear again, this time with a solution that re-awakens them. They do this because if a bear remains asleep during its long trip to the forest, it may inadvertently injure itself in its kennel or not be fully alert when it's set free.

It usually takes 10 to 15 minutes for a bear to fall asleep with the sedative, and another 10 to 15 minutes to reawaken with the reversing injection. However, before that happens, it falls on the shoulders— literally—of Nathan, Ciara, and several stronger-than-they-look interns to hoist the carefully locked steel kennel, with the bear inside, and carry it to the awaiting pickup truck using nothing but their grit, legs, and inner fortitude. It is a Herculean feat of strength, purpose, and dedication, but there's no other way to do it.

Then it's good-bye time. The bears whom Critter Care took care of so lovingly, patiently, and selflessly for up to a year are finally about to do what Critter Care hopes all its guests will do: live in the wilderness again, where they belong.

Even so, there's tension in the air. As April's chapter explained, Critter Care and other animal-welfare groups in BC have an unhappy relationship with the province's Conservation Officer Service. Critter Care is permitted to release other species of animals into the wild, but because of a provincial law, they don't include bears. So on release days, it's not Critter Care staff who will drive the bears back to their homes, but the same conservation officers who might have shot and killed their mothers. It's an irony that irks Dr. Macquisten. "Seventy percent of these bears are here because their mothers were killed by [the COs]," he says. "But because of groups like Critter Care, this gives them an opportunity to look good—to show that they care about conservation, too."

Conflicting emotions also play a role. Ciara calls the moment bittersweet. As glad as she is to see the bears return to the forest, these are the same bears she and other staff and interns once cradled in their arms and nursed with a bottle. How can she not be sad to see them go? But mainly, it's a "relief," she says. And she means it. After all, at its busiest, Critter Care had 29 bears to care for, and that's too many to look after at once.

And don't forget, the next two have arrived already.

JUVENILE DELINQUENTS

WHEN A BABY raccoon arrives at Critter Care, it either goes to Lynda Brown's house or to the society's nursery where it's fed, burped, and made to feel safe. However, when the raccoon is older, it's moved to a new place jokingly called the JD Room—JD for "Juvenile Delinquents." In the JD Room are two stalls, each about the size of a garden shed, with carpets, toys, food bowls, an open window and, crucially, a pan of water.

When raccoons enter these stalls at around five to six weeks old, they get to stretch their slightly longer legs, learn about temperature change thanks to the open window, and, just like a human toddler, are potty trained. When interns stimulate them to pee and poo, they place the animals' hind legs in the pan of water so they learn to associate relieving themselves with water, the way wild raccoons do. Then, after about a week, the young raccoons are moved to an outdoor enclosure, where they'll remain until they're released.

This furry rascal got his leg caught in a soccer net. But in a day, he was fine and ready to hit the pitch again.

JULY

JUNE ENDED WITH bears so perhaps it's fitting that July begins with them. Two more cubs have arrived, bringing the new total to four... so far.

The month's most extraordinary story, also so far, belongs to Meatloaf, a grossly overweight squirrel. In the wild, a big squirrel might weigh as much as 700 grams (25 ounces). Meatloaf weighs twice that. At least she did when she arrived with her equally overweight sister. Unfortunately, her sister's health was so badly impacted by her obesity that she died soon after arriving at Critter Care. Meatloaf is now on a diet and is already 100 grams (3.5 ounces) lighter. But she still has a long way to go.

When Meatloaf and her sister were babies, they were adopted as pets by a couple who spoiled them rotten with peanuts, granola, trail mix, and other fattening delicacies. They would have carried on doing so had they not decided to move out of the province. BC provincial law forbids people from taking wildlife over borders, so the two squirrels came to Critter Care instead. O'Higgins had never seen anything like them. Meatloaf is the critter equivalent of the Michelin Man.

Meatloaf gets weighed once a week, and over time it's turned into quite an ordeal—in a good way. She used to be easy to grab, but now when her "co-parents" Sophia Hertel and Emma Robson,

This grossly overweight squirrel, brought up as a domestic pet and fed a crazy diet of junk food, weighs twice what even the biggest squirrel should weigh. No wonder staff have named her Meatloaf.

the interns charged with caring for her, enter her pen, she skitters around like a ricocheting bullet trying to evade them. This is exactly what she should do as a squirrel, an animal other kinds of animals often want to eat.

The news from the scale is also good. After another seven days, she's down to 1,030 grams (36 ounces). She's still far too heavy, but this is definitely another step in the right direction. Right now, her main problem is the folds of loose skin she's carrying. She looks more like a flying squirrel than a terrestrial one. Ciara hopes

that with time they'll shrink along with the rest of her body, but if they don't, she may require a "tummy tuck." That's right, plastic surgery. It's not just for humans anymore.

While Meatloaf's is an extreme case, it's not that unusual for people to adopt wild babies thinking they can turn them into pets. Nathan recalls one raccoon who was brought up on marshmallows and Cheese Whiz. Yet he not only survived, he was eventually made well enough to be released into the wild like any other raccoon. Nathan has also seen bunnies and squirrels raised on chocolate milk and whipped cream. Why whipped cream? Because somewhere on the Internet is an untrue and misleading article that claims whipped cream is good for wild animals. It's not, but as we all know, if it's on the Internet, someone somewhere will believe it.

Actually, the biggest news of the moment is the sheer number of animals Critter Care has had to deal with this year: 1,487 as of July 14. Last year they looked after 1,794 in total.

To have reached almost the same number in half the time is unprecedented and terribly worrying for everyone.

THERE IS also a new coyote on site who may or may not prove to be a friend for Lucifer. She's a month younger than he is and that may be too much of an age gap for them to become friends. Time will tell. Staff are going to let them get to know each other slowly through a fence. If things look promising, the fence will come down. If not, each will have their own space. For his part, Lucifer is now eating food with fur on it—rabbits. He used to eat steak, but if he's going to make it in the wild one day, he has to learn that dinner isn't served on a platter. Not anymore.

A week later, and it no longer matters if Lucifer and the still unnamed female will get along because he's been let go. Staff felt it was time, and it was. At first, he was so nervous that Ciara had to tilt his kennel to force him out. But as soon as his paws hit the ground, he was gone, charging into the forest like a deer. And speaking of, two fawns have also been released with similar set-me-free zest.

Another bear has also arrived, bringing the total to five. This one is a young male who had an open wound on one of his hind legs. A veterinarian painstakingly cleaned and closed the wound with stitches, which the cub promptly tore out the next day. Never mind, Ciara says, the wound isn't infected so he ought to be fine.

There's also been a tragedy in the otter enclosure. One of Dame's pups, Custard, has drowned in a pool, and even worse, it's likely that Dame was the one who drowned him. She may have found that at her age she was unable to feed him

Critter Care staff were hoping for a rest after looking after so many bears over the last 12 months. But no such luck. By the end of July, they have six new ones to care for, including this cub.

and his brother Jam satisfactorily, so, as horrific as it sounds, she may have sacrificed one to sustain the other. Such are nature's cruel calculations sometimes. As a result, Jam will now live with Critter Care's nine other otter pups while Dame will live alone.

▲ These otter pups are exactly where they want to be—on dry land. But Critter Care staff have other ideas for them.

➤ You wouldn't think a river otter would need to be taught how to swim. But they do...and they often don't like it. Here, Nathan Wagstaffe introduces one such reluctant pupil to the wonderful world of water.

BY THE THIRD week of July, most of Critter Care's raccoons and skunks are in outdoor enclosures and on the final leg of their journey back to nature. The nursery that was once crawling with their tiny helpless bodies is almost empty. A second wave of squirrel babies is expected at any time, but it won't be as overwhelming as the first. The year is marching on.

Evidence of that is that soon it will be time for Nathan to start teaching Critter Care's 10 otter pups how to swim. Yes, surprising as that sounds, even otters have

to learn to swim, like children. Meantime, Nathan has placed two baby pools in their enclosure so they can literally get their feet wet. Also like children, some take to the water like, well, otters, while others are as disdainful of it as cats. But thanks to Nathan, by the time they leave Critter Care, each and every one of them will know how to swim. They'll have to if they're going to survive the great outdoors.

So a week later, Nathan and otter intern Mark Sheridan bring seven of the 10 otter pups (the other three are still too little) to Critter Care's Otter Spa, an enclosure with a metre-deep pool in it. The otters are instantly curious. They have never been to the spa, so it's of immense interest. Except for the pool, that is, which they are not keen on at all.

They're all brave enough to stick their faces in it, but that's it. They're happy to run around the pool's concrete edge and smell all the new smells the spa has to offer. But swimming? No thanks. It's up to Mark and Nathan to pick them up and place them—often kicking and complaining—in the water one by one. All of them have an innate ability to swim. None is going to drown. But none of them likes it, and every single one climbs back onto the pool's edge as quickly as they can.

Mother otters show little mercy when teaching their offspring to swim. They drag their beleaguered pups into the water again and again and again until they learn. And that's that. No argument. Nathan and Mark are considerably gentler, but the principle is the same. As soon as a pup has hauled itself out of the pool, they lift it back in. Sometimes they place their hands under its belly to give it a sense of security. But there's no such thing as "this isn't for you," because if you're an otter and you can't swim, you can't live.

It usually takes a week or two of daily lessons for the pups to finally get, ahem, into the swim of things. Then there's no

It's July, so Critter Care's raccoon kits are getting their first taste of the outdoors … which is where they'll be released when their time comes.

stopping them. They'll remain in the spa until they're released, either in the fall or next spring. Before that happens, they'll also have to learn to fish. That's their next challenge.

As it's July, it's hot. Too hot. Staff try to keep the animals cool by soaking and freezing towels, and then throwing them in the animals' enclosures. They also freeze bowls of fruit and water like Popsicles. One intern's specialty is frozen kibble and peanut butter. What the animals really want is shade, but that's hard to come by when you're not in a forest.

Finally, a sixth bear cub has arrived. A female this time. July ends as it began, with bears. Full circle.

A SURPRISING SOCCER STAR

WHEN IT COMES to urban wildlife, few species are as successful as coyotes. They've adapted to city living as comfortably as we have. But even they get into trouble now and then. On a school soccer field not far from Critter Care, a coyote pup is found with his foreleg caught in a goal net. As a result, it's swollen like a balloon. But when he's freed and brought to Critter Care, it deflates like one too. His stay is short. In just two days he's back where he was found, the net conspicuously gone. The school is in a neighbourhood where numerous coyote pups have been sighted. Obviously this four-legged Lionel Messi was one of them.

Bear cubs continue to be brought to Critter Care's gates by conservation officers who've killed their mothers. As it's August, this one gets the pleasure of tucking into a watermelon . . . as long as he can figure out how to crack it open.

AUGUST

BEARS, *AGAIN*. Actually just one, but she is the sister of the cub who arrived at the end of July. Both are well, but there's something fishy about the situation. Both were trapped by COs simultaneously, but they arrived at Critter Care five days apart. Why? Not only that, COs won't say why they killed their mother, but Critter Care would like to know.

Meantime, more and more animals are being released or readied for release. In just over a week, all the fawns will be let go. There are hardly any skunks left, and most of the raccoons will be gone by the end of September. The only animals coming in are baby squirrels and a few young rabbits injured by cats or dogs.

And speaking of squirrels, Meatloaf just keeps getting thinner. She's moving much better, too. She climbs like she's flying, and despite having lived with people for 18 months, she's becoming increasingly wary of them. That's essential for the survival of any wild animal. The folds of skin that concerned O'Higgins still flap about her like Batman's cape, but given how well she moves, it looks as if plastic surgery won't be necessary after all.

In the pool, the otter pups are finally doing what adult otters do so gracefully and proficiently: they're swimming. Mark and another intern, Laura Hardiman, no longer have to lift them into the water. Instead, they simply open the carriers they're

All those swimming lessons have paid off. Critter Care's otter pups are now naturals in the water. And who doesn't like a waterslide?

transported in and wait. And eventually, given sufficient time and curiosity, they all slip into the water voluntarily. Okay, a couple still need a nudge or two, but only a nudge. And they stay in the pool, too.

When they do get out, the first thing they do is dry themselves on a towel. Seriously. Just like a person. There are towels lying flat all around the pool, and the otters rub themselves on them until their silky walnut fur is dry again. By a

river, they'd use leaves, grass, and even rocks, but the intent is the same. Otters are very clean, says Mark, so for them grooming is natural. They always want to look their best.

DAYS AFTER their arrival, new information about the bear cubs emerges. According to the conservation officers who trapped them, one of the cubs became entangled in a soccer net on someone's property. When a CO stepped in to rescue her, the mother bear charged. So the CO shot her in the face with a beanbag, rendering her unconscious. The cubs were then trapped and removed, and the mother was left where she was overnight in pain. The next day, it seemed as if she still hadn't recovered, so the COs put her down.

The COs planned to deliver both cubs to Critter Care, but somehow, one of the cubs got away, and that's why they arrived almost a week apart. But the most pressing question remains why the COs killed their mother. Couldn't they have given her more time to recover and then re-establish the family? They don't seem to think so.

When it's time to release the society's fawns, 11 staff and interns gather in the fawns' enclosure before dawn on a Thursday to lift five frightened, kicking animals—who can weigh about 20 kilograms (44 pounds) each—and carry them to five transport crates. It's exhausting work, but someone's got to do it.

The plywood crates, which are slightly larger than a doghouse, require tremendous strength to lift empty. With a fawn inside, they are like carrying blocks of lead. Two of the fawns, a brother and sister, will be released together. The rest will go it alone.

Animal care supervisor Cayce Anderson, an intern named Nora Hoffman, and maintenance man Lachie Herford are assigned the siblings. Cayce won't say where they're going, but she, Nora, and Lachie—all

August is usually when orphaned animals prepare to leave Critter Care, not make it their new home. Baby squirrels, however, are exceptions because squirrel mothers often have two litters a year.

armed with bug spray, sunscreen, hats, and boots—will drive for hours, park, and then heave the weighty transport crates, one at a time, through dense bush for twenty minutes. They chose the spot because they know, thanks to Google Earth, that it's rich in things that deer love: willows, fruit trees, berry bushes, and natural cover. And they were right. Both fawns are gone in minutes.

▲ This brother-and-sister pair of fawns have been packed into a crate and loaded onto a truck. It's the last they'll see of Critter Care because they're on their way to their future—in the wild.

➤ You can see the uncertainty on this fawn's face as she takes her first wary step into her new forever home... the big wide—and unknown—wilderness.

Critter Care is equally vigilant when choosing release spots for other animals so they will be let out in the best habitat for them. Skunks, for example, need plenty of water, soft ground to dig in, and hollow logs to hide in. When it's their turn to be released, the result is the same as with the deer: They too go like a shot.

And yes, just as with the bears, "it's bittersweet," says Cayce, but also eminently right. "It means so much to see

them in the wild doing what they should do and being where they should be. It's really wonderful."

Thanks to these releases, Critter Care would be looking pretty empty now if it weren't for the 104 raccoons still on site. As mentioned earlier, staff hope to release them in six weeks, but that depends on how much weight they gain. Young raccoons are unique among all Critter Care orphans in that they can lose up to half their body weight when they're released. Yes, living free is exciting after being cooped up in a Critter Care cage for months, but it can also be stressful and challenging. Adapting to life outside requires lots of moving around, which requires lots of calories. And even though Critter Care raccoons do learn how to forage for food to replenish those calories, it can be hard to figure out at first.

In the middle of August, another disturbing milestone is reached. Critter Care has now surpassed the total number of animals it took in last year—1,793— which until now was the busiest year it had ever had. Then, as if to emphasize the point, seven juvenile opossums arrive when their mother and a sibling are killed by a car. Each one isn't much bigger than a small rat, but given that they began life the size of a jellybean, that represents quite a growth spurt.

By the third week of August, it's time to let Meatloaf go. At 754 grams, she's

still heavy and her skin still folds around
her like a set of drapes, but she moves
well, she's wary of people, and she's ready.
So, finally, she's set free in a forested area
northeast of Vancouver. First, she climbs a
tree, then she sits on a branch for a while
to look around, and then she disappears.
And one of Critter Care's most bizarre tales
is over.

JULY'S CHAPTER touched on how people
like the couple who adopted Meatloaf will
sometimes attempt to turn baby wildlife
into pets. A far more common practice,
says Cayce, is people "rescuing" wildlife
when it isn't in danger. You already know
how people can sometimes mistakenly
believe that solitary fawns are abandoned
when their mothers leave them to feed.
Any aquarium will tell you that the same
thing happens to baby seals. Because of
this, whenever anyone phones Critter Care
about what might look like an orphaned
animal, they're always asked to wait a day
to make sure that the baby's mother really
is gone.

It turns out more baby rabbits are
"rescued" this way than any other kind
of animal. It's easy to see why—it's truly
hard to imagine anything cuter or more
vulnerable than a three-week-old bunny.
They literally are no bigger than a human
baby's shoe. So, for us, it's inconceivable to
think of a creature that small and helpless
surviving alone in the large and perilous

There's a reason people say rabbits breed like rabbits . . . because they do. Some mothers have up to 12 litters a year. So Critter Care is never short of their ultra-adorable offspring.

wilderness. In fact, most don't. They usually become a larger animal's dinner. Yet three weeks is when mother rabbits wean their babies and turf them out of the nest. Even when they're still in the nest, they only see their mother twice a day because that's how often she returns from foraging to feed them. While their mothers are away, they, like fawns, are left scentless on their own.

With our own protective instincts triggered so urgently at the sight of such helpless-looking creatures, is it any wonder that we try to "rescue" so many of them? But part of nature's balance are its food chains, and bunnies are at the bottom of them, which is why so many are born. That's another reason why leaving them where they are is essential.

However, while disturbing them unnecessarily is undeniably wrong, it is also understandable. Critter Care is ending August with three baby rabbits in its care, and you'd have to be a snowman for the sight of them not to melt your heart.

ALL WASHED UP

BY MID-AUGUST, ALL of the society's raccoons are living in outdoor enclosures and learning to forage for their food. They have to dig in the dirt to find grubs and slugs. They're also given whole branches of them from which they have to learn to pick edible berries. And they always have water nearby because they like to soak their food before they eat it. In fact, the German word for raccoon, *waschbär*, means "washing bear."

Except it's a myth. While it may look as if raccoons wash their food, what they're really doing is stimulating the nerve endings in their hands by wetting them so they have a better idea of what they're about to eat. Because despite the big spectacles they wear, raccoons actually have rather poor vision.

Mustard is one of only two otters whom otter tech Nathan Wagstaffe has deemed fit for release this year. The others are still too immature, he says.

SEPTEMBER

YOU KNOW FALL is on its way when someone's left a dozen cartons of fresh apples outside Critter Care's nursery. The society's bears will certainly enjoy those.

For kids, September is a time of beginnings. New teachers, friends, classes. At Critter Care, it's the opposite: a time of good-byes. The skunks and fawns are already gone. Now it's the raccoons' turn. The first week of the month saw 31 leave. Forty more will depart the week after, followed by the final 10 in October. Those left behind will stick around until spring.

But raccoon releases are different from others because, of all the animals Critter Care looks after, they are the only ones who seem reluctant to leave. It's hard to say why, but Cayce believes it's because they're intelligent enough to realize what a sea change freedom represents. As the previous chapter explained, it's a formidable challenge. There's no one to look after them anymore, and that can be terrifically hard. So, to make their departure easier, raccoons are never released by the intern who nursed them. In the raccoons' eyes, that person is like their mother, providing them with all the food and comfort they need, so why would they want to leave them?

They also tend to linger where they're let go. As August's chapter explained, Critter Care is extra careful about where it releases all its animals, and raccoons are no exception. It has to

Marmalade is also ready to go, says Wagstaffe. It's no wonder. Of all the otter pups Critter Care took in this year, Marmalade has always been head girl.

be a place with big bushes they can hide in, trees they can climb, soil they can dig and water. The last thing raccoons learn at Critter Care is how to fish. Live guppies are put in containers of water and the raccoons are encouraged to catch them. As well, staff and interns won't leave them until they've seen the raccoons scale a tree, scrounge in the soil, and maybe grab a fish.

They're also released in groups. The eight raccoons who shared a Critter Care cage are always released together. Sometimes they stick together and sometimes they amble off on their own. But they never bolt like a fawn or a squirrel. Instead, they take their time, as if they're taking stock. Some even try to return to the kennels they were sprung from, because they seem to know that—good or bad—this is it. From now on, they're the real thing: wildlife.

IT ISN'T just the raccoons that are leaving, though. Incredibly, Miss Dame, the ancient otter the society rescued late last year, has flown the coop. She climbed the fence that surrounded her enclosure (*a fence topped with barbed wire*) and then shimmied down the other side to what she evidently longed for: freedom. Staff, who were as stunned by her escape as they've been by anything in years, were only able to figure out what

Mustard and Marmalade are still enjoying the home they've had since they were babies. But all that will change next month.

happened thanks to a tuft of fur left behind on one of the barbs.

They searched for her in the vain hope of bringing her back, but she had vanished. Eventually a couple of passers-by spotted her by a river fishing (something Nathan didn't think she was capable of) and, according to them, looking fine. She's been seen a couple more times since, and again, according to reports, appeared to be managing perfectly. It's more than astonishing. When she was rescued last December, she was barely alive, thin as a daffodil stem, and with teeth so worn she had to eat pablum. It was only because of the root canals she had done that she

was able to eat fish. No one thought for a moment that she would ever live in the wild again.

But content as she seemed to be swimming in her own pool with food delivered regularly on a platter, it turns out what she really wanted was to be free. And now she is. Staff are understandably worried about how she'll survive the winter, but at the same time, they're trying to be philosophical. After all, they want their animals to be happy. And if this is what makes Miss Dame happy, then who are they to stop her?

As Cayce puts it: "We're happy that we know she's out there and doing well."

Maybe it makes sense. Dame lived her

Most of Critter Care's animals can't wait to return to the big wide world. Not raccoons. They take their time. It's as if they know living wild won't bring roses every day, and that from now on, no one will be looking after them. And that's kinda scary.

THE FIRST day of fall is partly sunny and cooler. Summer's scorching heat is spent, and the trees are well on their way to changing costume from green to red, gold, amber, and russet. At Critter Care, despite having admitted a record 2,104 animals so far this year (with more than three months to go!), fall means a gradual slowing down. Instead of hundreds of animals demanding care at precisely the same time, there are now just over 80. The odd infant squirrel still turns up with some regularity, and last week a young beaver named Mabel was found crying in a river by a man in a boat. She is a hissing, spitting, feisty thing who is not at all happy about being caged, but she's too small to let go before spring. The furious, frenzied pace of baby season, however, seems to be over. Fingers crossed.

The otters' fishing lessons are set for the last Friday in September, but drenching rains delay them again by preventing delivery of a key component—the fish! And when they finally do commence two days later, there are only two pupils, Mustard, a male, and Marmalade, a female. The other seven, says Nathan, are too small, too immature, or both. By immature, he means they're not behaving as would-be wild otters should. Like children, all they want to do is play, and they still enjoy human company, a pleasure too dangerous for any wild creature to indulge. So all of them, including Jam and Scone, will remain at Critter Care until spring.

whole life as a wild animal, so in her heart that's what she will always be. Also, given that she's so close to Critter Care, if something does go wrong, perhaps she can be rescued a second time.

Speaking of otters, the pups at the society, including Dame's remaining son and daughter, Jam and Scone, were supposed to have begun fishing lessons this week, but their pool is leaking so the lessons have had to be postponed.

The bear pen that Critter Care had built in February has been complete for a few months now. Good thing, too, because sadly, there's been no let-up in the number of orphaned bears it's been taking in.

By contrast, Mustard and Marmalade disdain human attention and can't wait to catch the goldfish Nathan has placed in a baby pool. But goldfish are small, slow-moving, and easy to nab. The otters' real test comes in a full-sized pool stocked with trout. In addition to being larger and stronger than goldfish, they're far quicker and more elusive, and they can change course in an instant like an NHL winger, making it hard to predict where they're going to go next.

The training pool is hexagonal, about 1.2 metres (four feet) wide and 2.4 metres (eight feet) deep. Otter intern Rachel Huang dumps four live trout into it and then invites Mustard and Marmalade to do their best. At first, they're far more interested in the bucket the trout arrived in than the fish themselves. But with time, Marmalade dives in and in pretty short order catches one. It takes her a few tries because the fish are fast and slippery, but given the limited size and depth of the pool, the trout don't stand a chance. However, even with this advantage, Marmalade is showing her mettle. Mustard, on the other hand, refuses even to get his whiskers wet. What

It's not easy catching a wild animal. Especially one who may be terrified and in pain. So here, interns Antonio De Rosa and Julia Rugheimer practise with a teddy bear. The idea is to lasso the animal around its neck and one paw. That way it won't choke.

he will do, however, is steal Marmalade's fish when she brings them on deck. That's not the way this is supposed to work!

After another day of lessons, nothing has changed. Marmalade, with her famously assertive take-charge, be-first personality (she would be captain of any school team she joined), continues to fish, and Mustard continues to watch. So steps must be taken. Rachel decides to

significantly reduce the amount of chicken and vegetables the otters usually receive to make Mustard hungrier—literally and figuratively. In other words, if he wants something to eat, he'll have to go and get it. But there's still plenty of time for him to learn, she advises. The otters have two or three more weeks of practice ahead of them, so things can only improve. And they will.

CATCH AS CATCH CAN

MAY'S CHAPTER EXPLAINED that sometimes animals are caught in traps. But in addition to ignoring laws that forbid setting traps in suburban areas, some people also fail to anchor the traps in the ground, meaning that when raccoons, coyotes, or skunks become ensnared in one, they will often tow it around frantically in a futile attempt to get free.

To capture these animals, Critter Care staff or interns literally have to lasso them with something called a catchpole. Picture the loop of a rope affixed to the end of a broom handle. But what makes the manoeuvre especially tricky is that the noose has to go around not just the animal's neck but a foreleg as well to avoid choking the animal while it struggles to escape. It's no easy feat, to say the least, so interns at Critter Care practise it regularly on stuffed teddy bears that are dragged around the compound on the end of a string. Further proof that there are few lengths Critter Care won't go to for the sake of its guests.

Bears may not know about Halloween, but they do know pumpkins taste good. This cub is discovering that as he bites into October's signature holiday treat for the first time.

OCTOBER

IVE DAYS INTO October, and Rachel still hasn't seen Mustard swim. She's seen him perched on the edge of the pool poking his nose in the water, and she's seen his fur dripping wet, which means he must have taken a plunge at some point. But she's never actually seen him enter the pool and move around in it. Not once in over a week. She doesn't know what to make of this, but her supervisors say there's no reason to worry—yet.

Needless to say, she also hasn't seen him fish, but to be fair, that's because there haven't been any fish for him—or Marmalade—to catch. The supplier is having problems delivering them. He promises to resolve them as quickly as he can, but until he does, all lessons are off. How can you hold a fishing lesson without fish? When Nathan returns from his holiday, Rachel hopes to put questions like this to him.

MEANWHILE, THE society has received two more orphaned bear cubs. Their mother was shot, tragically, by Conservation Officers. They felt she was an irredeemable problem bear that was teaching her cubs to forage for food in alleyways and people's backyards. But Critter Care founder Gail Martin has heard this explanation before. Now, Critter Care has nine bears to look after instead of seven. They arrived only three days ago so they haven't been

▲ They just keep coming. Conservation officers have shot another mother bear, so Critter Care has no choice but to welcome and look after her two offspring. That brings their bear total to nine—so far. Five are pictured here.

➤ Her fur prevents you from seeing it, but this skunk named Sunflower has a scar around the front part of her body from when she was trapped in a plastic cord. Fortunately someone saw she was suffering and brought her to Critter Care where they cut the cord and nursed her back to health. Now she's perfectly well and ready to be released.

named, but the others are Teller, Aurora, Luna, Blueberry, Dandelion, Remy, and Reema.

Then there is Sunflower, who is not a bear, but a skunk. A young skunk with a very bad injury. Somehow, when she was even younger, she managed to wrap a plastic cord around her neck and under one foreleg. And as she grew, the cord cut into her like a length of wire. Fortunately, someone noticed her having difficulty

crawling under his fence and called Critter Care. If he hadn't, they never would have known about her horrible suffering. But a week later, she's healing beautifully. Ciara expects her to recover completely, though she will always have a scar.

CANADIAN THANKSGIVING is coming, so to celebrate, the society's twelve interns are having a pie-baking contest. Each intern has an hour to bake a pie of their choice, with the winner chosen by their supervisors. There is also talk of a pie-eating contest to follow, but the rules are still being determined.

And speaking of volunteers, Norm Snihur, the now 82-year-old pilot who rescues wildlife with his helicopter, has been grounded due to hip surgery. In the month prior to his operation, he flew twenty-three hours rescuing distressed animals, but now it looks as if he won't be back in the air until next year. "I miss it already," he says forlornly.

As for non-human animals, the main headline in the middle of the month still belongs to Marmalade and Mustard, who are about to be released. Yes, Mustard has finally decided to do what all river otters are expected, even born, to do—swim and fish. He's doing both well enough that Nathan believes he's ready to live independently in the wild. He and Marmalade will be released together at a site Nathan is still scouting. For otters, that's somewhere remote, pristine, and, of course, watery. A river mouth is ideal because that way they can fish in both the river and whatever body of water it feeds. Marmalade and Mustard continue to gain more and more experience in the pool, but their days of fishing for specially bought trout in a purpose-built concrete tub are drawing to a close. Real life is about to dawn instead.

(However, to make the transition easier, the pair will be left with a few buckets of

food—different kinds of protein, as well as fruit and vegetables—in case they don't get the hang of feeding themselves right away.)

When the time finally comes for their departure, they are released at daybreak on a lakeshore hours away from Critter Care or anywhere else. In typical Marmalade fashion, she pours herself into the water the second she sees it, while Mustard, also true to form, decides to inspect the beach first. Soon enough, however, they're both frolicking in their new home. Then something odd happens. Mustard swims around a bend so Marmalade can't see him anymore and shrieks with alarm. Nathan, Mark, and Rachel, who are all there to say good-bye, direct her to her friend, and she's okay again. But they're all surprised

that it was Mustard who took the lead to go exploring.

Otters don't mate until they're two years old, meaning if Marmalade and Mustard do pair off, it won't be for another year and a half. But Nathan, a perpetual matchmaker, can't resist the prospect. "Maybe I'll be a granddad one day," he beams. Maybe he will. In the meantime, he plans to return in a few weeks to check up on them.

DURING THE same week as Marmalade and Mustard's release, 10 raccoons are also let go. Apart from seven squirrels who are waiting to be released on the next sunny day, the raccoons will be the last animals Critter Care bids farewell to this year. The society never releases animals in winter—it wants its guests to have the best, most advantageous start possible, and winter is when wildlife struggle the most.

That is, unless you're a bear, which, if it weighs enough, has the luxury of sleeping the winter away by living off its fat. Teller, Aurora, Luna, Blueberry, Dandelion, Remy, Reema, and the two newest arrivals, now named Tony and Elena, seem to be having sleepy thoughts already and it's only October. They're not nearly as active nor as hungry as they were in spring and summer, so it won't be long before staff halve the amount of food they're given, and then halve it again in December. Except by then, the bears probably won't need it. Instead, they'll be tucked away in their dens, curled up in cozy clutches of two, three, and four, dreaming of whatever bears dream of. Maybe a forest to explore, berries to savour, or salmon to catch.

Also staying for the winter will be Mabel, the young beaver with the rebellious attitude to match (although that's improving). She's been moved to the enclosure where Marmalade and Mustard spent their last days, although she's not allowed near the pool where they fished. Staff aren't confident enough of her swimming skills to permit an unsupervised dip. But, being a beaver, she makes good use of the

◄ This young female beaver was found crying in a river by a man in a boat. She has since been named Mabel and will be spending the winter at Critter Care where they will give her plenty of wood so she can practise building a lodge.

▲ This is it—Marmalade's and Mustard's first taste of freedom, and they they can't wait.

wood she's given, building and rebuilding her approximation of a lodge and dam. Or as Ciara describes it: "She's redecorating daily."

By the end of the month, the last squirrels are gone and so is Sunflower, the skunk who arrived with a plastic cord wrapped around her neck and front paw. Her injury was one of the worst Ciara had ever seen. If the man hadn't called Critter Care about her, she would have undoubtedly died—slowly and painfully. Instead, after making an amazingly swift recovery,

she's back living near where she was found. As this chapter mentioned earlier, she'll always have a scar, but otherwise she's fine. So well, in fact, that as a parting gift, she couldn't resist doing what all skunks do to people who dare to come too close. (Fortunately, Ciara ducked in time.) Talk about biting the hand that feeds you.

And Christmas has come early to the society's bears. Every year, a nearby Christmas tree farm donates trees that the bears use to block entrances to their dens when they're ready to go to sleep. The

If Mustard and Marmalade ever wondered why it was so important for them to learn to swim, now they know. Their new home is by a lake hours away from Critter Care. But Wagstaffe vows he'll be back to visit them.

only condition is that Nathan cuts them down himself. So he has, and good thing too, because the bears look more and more ready to bid the year goodnight. They're only eating a quarter (or less) of what they used to, and staff hardly ever see them anymore. Ciara reckons they'll be out cold by mid-November.

And no, irresistible as the idea may seem, even though they're Christmas trees, no one decorates them. Remember, Critter Care dedicates itself to mimicking nature as faithfully as possible, and in the forest—at least as far as anyone knows—nature has never seen fit to hang a bauble or a star on a spruce or a fir. Even on December 25.

TOUGH AS NAILS

ONE OF CIARA'S sadder duties this month is to euthanize an old raccoon who was brought in with a spinal injury that made using her hind legs impossible. But what was remarkable about her was that she only ever had one front leg. Just as humans can be born with physical deformities, so can animals.

The difference is that there is no one to help the animals on their way, meaning that for this raccoon's whole life—and by raccoon standards it was a long one—she managed valiantly on just three legs. It goes to show that even animals have to play the cards they're dealt.

Thumbelina came by her name honestly. When she arrived at Critter Care this month, she weighed only five kilos (11 pounds), despite being 11 months old. Now she's making up for those hungry months by eating as much as she wants. She couldn't ask for a better early Christmas present.

NOVEMBER

ANOTHER MONTH, another bear, or so it must seem sometimes. This one's name is Thumbelina, which should tell you everything you need to know about how big—or small—she is. Actually, at just under five kilograms (11 pounds), it would be fair to say she's tiny. A lot of housecats weigh more. And yet she's almost a year old. January's chapter mentioned a bear named Roxxy, who weighed only seven kilograms (16 pounds) when she was rescued the day after Christmas. She was a year old, too, but thanks to her amazing innate ability to remain small *and* alive even though there wasn't enough food for her to grow, she survived long enough to be rescued and eventually released. Thumbelina is the same. She probably was born in January of this year, separated from her mother soon after, and left alone. So she didn't grow, but like Roxxy, she didn't die either.

Now she's living—and growing, at last—in what June's chapter called the JD (Juvenile Delinquent) Room, a stall meant for juvenile raccoons on their way to moving outdoors. Critter Care's 29 raccoons are all housed outside now, so the stall is empty and perfect for a black bear runt who's getting a second chance at life thanks to reliable helpings of rice, a protein shake, strawberries, grapes, and regular (for now) doses of banana-flavoured antibiotics she needs for a mild infection. And yes, she will remain awake all winter.

This opossum was brought to Critter Care by a farmer who accused him of hunting his chickens. Critter Care staff suspect he was more interested in their eggs, but regardless of the truth, it's lucky for the opossum that the farmer let him live.

Not so the society's other nine bears, who now eat only every other day, and sleep many more hours than they remain awake. When they are awake, it's mainly to prepare their dens for their long winter's nap. In addition to the Christmas trees Nathan brought them last month, they like to cozy up their quarters with heaps of hay. When they finally do drift off for their big sleep—probably by month's end—it will be in a densely packed nest of pine boughs, hay, and bear fur, where they will be, to all intents and purposes, invisible to the outside world. Just as they would be in nature.

HOWEVER, IT'S not just the bears who are girding themselves for December, January, and February. With temperatures dropping to freezing some nights, staff and interns have been winterizing the raccoons' enclosures, too. Each shed is covered in blankets and has its own heat lamp. They're also wrapping the society's water pipes with insulation to keep them from freezing (unfortunately that's rarely foolproof) and storing rubber hoses indoors with heat lamps, too. Because with all the cleaning Critter Care does each day, being without hoses would render it akin to a horse with three legs. It could still move, but much more slowly.

November is grim in Metro Vancouver. It's the wettest, greyest, and arguably most depressing month of the year. So to cheer up the place, staff at Critter Care have decided to bring out some early Christmas decorations. There's a small twinkly tree in the reception room, a string of coloured lights around the main door, and red ribbons spiralling bannisters. They may not be able to do anything about the weather, but inside, they've definitely brightened the place up.

Mabel, the beaver, has received an early Christmas present, too. The door to her swimming pool is now open, so she's free to take a dip whenever she pleases. But only during the day. It's shut at night. Now if only she had some company.

After a couple of weeks, Thumbelina is off her antibiotics. Her infection has cleared, so she's eating normally and gaining weight. That means she's also off the protein shake, which was never intended for bears. Instead, she's adjusting to a diet more typical of bruins: fruits and vegetables. Bears are so big, strong, and

A chipmunk like this one has been brought in with a curious wound on his face and a pair of bright red eyes. Veterinary technicians hope eye drops will take care of them.

potentially dangerous (those sharp claws and enormous teeth) that it surprises many people to learn they're mainly vegetarian. That changes during the autumn salmon runs, when they can't get enough of the big oily fish. But in spring and summer, their diet consists mainly of plants. Yes, they'll happily turn over a log and slurp up all the bugs underneath, and if they live by the

No matter the month, Critter Care can pretty much count on having a squirrel to care for… or two or five. This one has learned that for the time being nourishment comes from a plastic tube.

sea, they'll swallow clams and mussels with a gourmand's gusto. They'll even scarf down barnacles like popcorn. But they're not the carnivores that wolves and cougars are. Providing the helping is big enough, they're perfectly happy with salad for dinner and berries for dessert.

Then—wouldn't you know it?—it happens again. In the third week of November, another orphaned cub is rescued. Though he's not as small as Thumbelina—29 kilograms (65 pounds) versus Thumbelina's five—he, like her,

was born last winter, was orphaned, and is seriously underweight as a result. Strangely, he was found on a dyke near a large swath of farmland. There wasn't a forest in sight. So how he got there is anyone's guess. Never mind. What matters is that Nathan and Laura, who has graduated from intern to full-time employee, got him out together with a couple of COs.

Unfortunately, the operation was anything but textbook. When one of the COs aimed to tranquilize the cub, he misfired and got him in a front paw

By November, baby season should be well and truly over, which means Critter Care can devote more of its time to helping distressed adults, such as this skunk caught in a very nasty looking trap.

instead of his shoulder. Even worse, the dart pierced an artery, which meant the poor cub bled something awful. Nathan and Laura wrapped his paw in gauze and tape and carried him in a blanket to a CO van, which drove him to a veterinarian, who rebandaged his paw and prescribed antibiotics.

Despite the mishaps, when the cub is safe, Laura can't help but be heartened by the fact that she and Nathan got to work alongside the COs when they attended the bear. That rarely happens. But this time,

they acted as partners, Laura says, and that was a promising development. She hopes it will happen again.

Meanwhile an opossum accused of killing chickens (more likely he was after their eggs) has also taken up temporary residence at Critter Care (he has some mange and scabs that need looking after), as has a chipmunk with a curious wound on his face and a bright red eye. Drops should take care of that.

Nathan hasn't had a chance to visit Marmalade and Mustard yet, but the

As we all know, bears sleep away the winter. But before they shut their eyes in December, they have to ready their dens in November.

otters they left behind continue to reside in the "spa" where they learned to swim. They'll stay there until spring. As with the raccoon enclosures, there's now a heat lamp in their den, but given their double layer of fur, they scarcely need it. Besides, when they sleep, they huddle together in a big brown ball of cozy otterness.

All seven swim expertly now, to the point that some will chase tennis balls and rubber ducks as if they were fish, even though their real lessons won't begin until next year. They're also made to forage for their food sometimes. Interns assigned to take care of them will fill a kiddie pool with soil or leaves and then hide fish, vegetables, or fruit in it, which the otters have to find. They prefer fish over everything else, but for reasons known only to them they're also mad about peppers. What is different is that Nathan no longer visits them. Because he nursed them, they see him as their mother, so as hard as it is for him, he has to break that bond so they won't miss him when they leave.

NOVEMBER 30 dawns brilliantly sunny and relatively warm, which may account for why Critter Care's bears are still, albeit barely, awake. They continue to emerge intermittently from their dens for an occasional snack or pee, so it's clear they haven't quite settled yet. But they will.

Meanwhile, the bear cub rescued from the farm dyke is doing well and has been named Beary. A conservation officer asked his daughter's Grade 2 class for suggestions, and "Beary" was the name they all chose for him. It may be short on imagination, but it leaves no doubt about the type of animal he is.

Lastly, a pair of interns were sent to rescue a skunk caught in a window frame last week. The rescue was a success and the skunk is fine, but being a skunk, he had to leave his calling card. Back at the office, the interns' smell preceded their appearance by some distance.

BUILDING FOR THE FUTURE

IN THE INTRODUCTION, it was mentioned that there were 56 structures on the Critter Care property, but the past year has changed that. A new bear enclosure was built at the beginning of the year, and now a new nursery is being constructed for the hordes of raccoon babies that appear like blossoms each spring. Staff hope it'll be ready for next year's bloom. The current nursery is just too small. Given that baby raccoons have to be fed every three hours, interns are literally jammed into closets, beneath counters, and under tables to accommodate themselves, their charges, and their bottles. The new nursery will ease that crush. A new examination room has been approved for construction, too.

Like Thumbelina, who was rescued in November, Noel, named for the season, was discovered motherless in a garage after having survived the year without growing. But now, also like Thumbelina, he's making up for it with a generous Critter Care diet.

DECEMBER

AS YOU NOW know, the only expected occurrences at Critter Care are unexpected. Circumstances spin on a dime. All it takes is for somebody new to arrive, and what seemed certain is anything but.

Ask the bears. They should be asleep. And at last some are. Blueberry, Dandelion, Reema, Remy, Tony, and Elena have finally hit their hay-and-pine sacks for good. Staff may not see them again until March. Ordinarily, Teller, Aurora, and Luna would have cashed in their tickets to dreamland, too—but then Beary arrived.

Beary, you'll recall, is the orphaned cub who was rescued from a dyke on the edge of a farm in November. Since then, he's been eating like a buffalo. So he's grown—a lot. Enough to enable him to sleep away the winter, so staff would like him to join Teller, Aurora, and Luna in their den. That way, if more bears arrive, there will be space in other dens for them as well. But how would you like it if, just as you were about to turn down your bedcovers, you were asked to sleep with a stranger? You may not mind, but Teller, Aurora, and Luna do. Which is why instead of closing their eyes, they have them firmly fixed—on Beary.

It's not that there isn't enough space. The bears' dens are big enough to accommodate four yearling cubs. Each den is only the size of a tool shed, but because sleeping bear cubs like to curl up

▲ This is the spot where Miss Dame was last seen by some passers-by. She hasn't been seen since, but as one year rolls into the next, Critter Care staff and interns hope she's well, warm, and safe.

➤ It isn't just the staff and interns who get into the spirit of Christmas. This raccoon decided to find out what all the fuss was about, too.

in cozy bear bundles just like otters, there's room enough for everyone. So to staff, it makes sense to have Teller, Aurora, and Luna share their shed with Beary.

Try telling that to Teller, Aurora, and Luna, though. They've known each other for months and have spent the last four weeks outfitting their den with just the right patchwork of pine boughs and hay to make it the perfect haven for three drowsy amigos. Not four. And so, they remain defiantly encamped in one den while Beary settles in another. Let's hope he's comfortable, because he may end up spending the whole winter there.

And Thumbelina? Yes, she's been eating and growing, but remember she started at five kilograms, while Beary was 29. Even if she ate like two buffalos, she couldn't pack on enough weight to go three months without eating more. So, unlike the other bears, she'll be awake for most of the winter, getting bigger and bigger.

By mid-month, the stalemate is over. The bears have prevailed, and the staff have given up and given in. Teller, Luna, and Aurora will share one den and Beary will occupy another. Nathan expects Beary will be fine even if he's alone. After all, he'll be asleep. Meantime, when Teller, Luna, or Aurora happen to emerge from their den and see Beary, it's expected that everyone will be cordial to everyone else. Evidently, Christmas is not just a season of goodwill to humans, but to fellow bears, too.

And don't forget, when they do fall asleep, they'll disappear from view behind the pine branches and hay they've fashioned to block the entrances to their dens. No one will hear them either, because bears don't snore.

CRITTER CARE has also decided to do something exceptional this year. As you know, it never releases animals in winter. But because of an intern shortage, staff have decided to semi-release eight raccoons. What that means is that these raccoons have been let go at nearby sites equipped with feeding stations that Critter Care replenishes twice a week. So even in winter they'll always have enough to eat. It also means if one isn't doing well, he or she can be reclaimed and looked after. Nathan calls it a "half release."

And in case you were wondering, no one has seen hide nor hair of Miss Dame since she was spotted fishing near the Critter Care compound in September. So only she knows how she's doing. Too bad.

When Christmas finally arrives, it brings a kind of Disney movie miracle. Remember the two bear cubs in August who got caught in a soccer net? Their mother had been shot by two COs when they were trying to untangle the cubs, and the babies were then brought to Critter Care and named Tony and Elena. It turns

Unfortunately, Christmas isn't merry for everyone. Winter is the most difficult season of the year for animals, like this deer, which have to scrounge for what little food is left in the forest. To make matters worse, many does are pregnant in winter, meaning they're eating for two.

out the mother bear actually had three cubs with her, not two. The COs didn't mention the third cub because he disappeared before they could catch him. But when he turned up alone in a Vancouver suburb two days before Christmas, they insisted he was Tony and Elena's missing and still unnamed brother. Obviously, he'll share a den with them when he, too, is ready to go to sleep, which will be soon.

And if that weren't enough, another Thumbelina was discovered three days earlier in a garage. Named Noel for the

season, he weighed only eight kilograms (19 pounds) when he arrived at Critter Care, but like Thumbelina, he's eating—a lot—and will soon share a pen with her.

ON CHRISTMAS DAY, Critter Care is festooned with stockings, ribbons, lights, baubles, and a Christmas tree. But only six people are there to enjoy them, and when their work is done, they'll vanish like Santa's sleigh. Staff and interns only have to work a four-hour shift, unless there's an emergency, which can

It's empty now, but next spring this new nursery will be bursting with wildlife orphans and their caregivers. Because it's always growing, Critter Care is always a work in progress.

occur at any time, even on December 25. Fortunately, this year all is quiet. One of the interns present is Kate Sadowska, a Polish immigrant who lives with her partner, Chris, in Manitoba. Her university degree is in environmental conservation, so Christmas or not, she decided to put that degree to work at Critter Care for eight weeks over the winter.

Naturally, she's a little lonely without Chris and her family, but there's always Zoom and Netflix. And she's learning all the time. "I would like to help with everything, but I don't know everything," she says. "Every day I learn something new, and that's very interesting."

Not that there are many animals to learn from now. Aside from all the bears—13 now—the only animals on site are the otters (minus Marmalade and Mustard), five cages of raccoons, two opossums, and Mabel, the beaver. And, needless to say, none seems particularly bothered by the significance of the day. As long as they're fed, watered and cleaned up after, they're content. So Christmas is quiet for them.

On December 31, the last day of the year, records show that Critter Care admitted an astonishing 2,331 animals this year, making it by far the busiest year in the society's history. Last year, it looked after 1,793. That's an astounding increase of 538 animals. Why did this happen? Nathan believes it's a combination of factors, good and bad. The bad? The wilderness is always under threat, which means its residents are, too. And, unfortunately, that's unlikely to change unless humans do more to protect wild spaces.

And the good? He believes people are becoming more observant of their non-human neighbours, and therefore more compassionate towards them. As Nathan puts it: "I think, because of climate change and increasing concerns about the environment, people are becoming more conscious of wildlife. Every year, we see people wanting to help wildlife more and more." For this reason, he believes next year's number could rise even higher.

The morning of New Year's Eve dawns grey, gloomy, and drizzly, and stays that way. No new animals arrive, and only four people, including Nathan, hold the fort. But as on Christmas Day, they'll be gone as soon as their work is done.

The intervening week has brought two changes, though. First, Thumbelina and Noel now share a pen—warily. Each occupies his or her own kennel inside the pen as a hiding place from the other. Food is placed between the kennels so they have to venture out to eat it. But they do so carefully and individually. When one eats, the other watches, and vice versa. Even so, Nathan insists they'll make friends soon enough.

Second, Teller, Luna, and Aurora have demonstrated that animals can be just as unpredictable, capricious, and generous as people by deciding to let bygones be bygones by inviting Beary into their den after all. And Beary has accepted. So what can one say, except "Happy New Year to all, and to all bears, a good and peaceful night."

DREAMLAND DIFFERENCES

MANY PEOPLE CALL a bear's long winter nap hibernation. But while what bears do is very similar to hibernation, it's subtly different. True hibernators, such as bumblebees, snakes, bats, skunks, and groundhogs, sleep entirely through the winter without ever waking up. When they nod off, nothing rouses them. They're down for the count. What makes bears different is that they can and do wake up from time to time. For example, if a female bear is pregnant, she will wake up to give birth to her cubs, but then she'll go back to sleep. She'll still nurse them—she has to, or they'd starve—but for the most part she does it while she's asleep. Male bears have even been known to leave their dens now and then just to stretch their legs.

Biologists call what bears undergo "torpor" to distinguish it from true hibernation. However, like hibernation, torpor causes a bear's heartbeat and breathing to slow and their temperature to drop. They also stop peeing and pooing. Instead, they recycle some elements of their pee into protein. How's that for spinning straw into gold?

"Critter Care is meant to be," says Gail Martin, the society's founder. "There are other wildlife rehab centres, but there's no place exactly like us."

AFTERWORD

ANOTHER YEAR AT Critter Care is over, and there will never be another one like it. The characters who came through its doors have seen to that. Will there ever be another Miss Dame? Or Roxxy? Or Meatloaf? No, but equally memorable characters will take their places just as they have ever since Gail Martin and her husband, Richard, launched Critter Care in 1984. Gail knows that better than anyone, because, through it all, she's been its constant. That's why she believes it will always exist.

"Critter Care is meant to be," she says. "There is no other place for the animals we look after. If we closed down, where would they go? There is no other place, so we have to keep going. We have no choice."

Last year, Critter Care looked after 2,331 animals, a record. But Gail isn't surprised. "Every year, more and more people hear of us, as we're the only organization in southern BC that does what we do. So it only stands to reason that the numbers will grow. We're a victim of our own success."

But it isn't just that, she says. People's attitudes towards animals are very different from what they were in 1984. "Years ago, COs would shoot a mother bear with cubs and nobody would care. Now when it happens, they're furious. In fact, the concern over bears brings in more money than anything else. People love bears. And rabbits. They bring in a lot of money, too."

Good thing, because, as was mentioned in the introduction, running Critter Care isn't cheap. There are all those people to pay and animals to feed and equipment to fix or replace. "Yes, we continually have to fundraise. But we're very fortunate in that a lot of people are very generous," says Gail. "Companies are, too. We get grants to build things and people leave us money in their wills. A lot of people care, so a lot of people give."

People care enough to work at Critter Care, too, which is anything but easy. Gail, who's dedicated her life to it, knows that better than anyone. "You just do it. That's all I can say. You cope. Our business is totally different from any other any other business, except maybe a hospital. People who go into it know that. They have to realize the hard work that's going to be involved and the long hours. Some days they might be working 12 hours or even more."

Even so, applications arrive regularly from people all over the world who want to have the chance to work those hours because they love animals as much as Gail does and want to help and learn about them.

As Critter Care's captain, Gail has spent many sleepless nights worrying about the stability of her ship and what would happen to it and its passengers if it foundered. Not anymore. "Gone are the days when I worried myself sick. It's a journey. I see that now. And like any other journey, you take it one step at a time. That means dealing with things as they come.

"What makes things a lot easier is that it's established now. People know about it, and I have good staff and good volunteers working for it. So I don't worry like I used to.

"As I said before, Critter Care is meant to be. There are other wildlife rehab centres, but there's no place exactly like us. So it's meant to be, and knowing that, you just have to keep going. Of course, it's the animals who do it for me. I couldn't begin to tell you about the thousands of animals I've been able to hold and care for since 1984. Most people will never have the kind of experiences I've had. Many people wouldn't want to have them, but it's something I have to do. I've always felt that way. And thanks to my husband, Richard, we made it happen. It's been wonderful."

ACKNOWLEDGEMENTS

THIS BOOK COULD not have been written without the endless help, cooperation, and patience of the staff, interns, and volunteers at Critter Care. Thank you for everything you do for the animals and everything you did for me.

SOURCES AND RECOMMENDED READING

SOURCES

PUBLISHER'S NOTE: Most of the information in this book was collected through personal interviews between the author and staff at the Critter Care Wildlife Society. Additional sources are listed below.

"American Black Bear," International Association for Bears, accessed July 22, 2021, bearbiology.org/bear-species/american-black-bear/.

"Beaver," Hinterland Who's Who, accessed July 22, 2021, hww.ca/en/wildlife/mammals/beaver.html.

CBC News, "Freezing bear cub was covered in ice after conservation officer dropped it off, concerned rescue group says," Jan 17, 2020, cbc.ca/news/canada/british-columbia/bear-cub-ice-conservation-officer-bc-1.5430432.

"Conservation Officer Service," Province of British Columbia, accessed July 22, 2021, gov.bc.ca/gov/content/environment/natural-resource-stewardship/natural-resource-law-enforcement/conservation-officer-service.

"Conservation Officer," Province of British Columbia, accessed July 22, 2021, gov.bc.ca/gov/content/careers-myhr/all-employees/pay-benefits/salaries/salarylookuptool/bcgeu-jobs/conservation-officer.

"Deer in the Capital Region," Capital Regional District, accessed July 22, 2021, crd.bc.ca/docs/default-source/regional-planning-pdf/Regional-Deer-Management/deerinthecapitalregion-web.pdf?sfvrsn=11a764ca_6.

"Do Bears Actually Hibernate?" Science World, accessed July 22, 2021, scienceworld.ca/stories/do-bears-actually-hibernate/.

"Eastern Cottontail Rabbit," Invasive Species Council of BC, accessed July 22, 2021, bcinvasives.ca/invasives/eastern-cottontail-rabbit/.

"Human-Wildlife Conflict," Province of British Columbia, accessed July 22, 2021, gov.bc.ca/gov/content/environment/plants-animals-ecosystems/wildlife/human-wildlife-conflict.

Lindores, Sharon. "Bryce Casavant, who refused to kill bear cubs, removed from Conservation Service," CBC, Aug 28, 2015, cbc.ca/news/canada/british-columbia/bryce-casavant-who-refused-to-kill-bear-cubs-removed-from-conservation-service-1.3207486.

Little, Simon. "B.C. couple who helped rescue emaciated bear cub won't face legal action," Global News, January 13, 2020, globalnews.ca/news/6407302/anmore-couple-bear-rescue-no-legal-action/.

"Losing their homes because of the growing needs of humans," World Wildlife Foundation, accessed July 22, 2021, wwf.panda.org/discover/our_focus/wildlife_practice/problems/habitat_loss_degradation.

"Management Plan for the Grey Wolf (Canis lupus) in British Columbia," B.C. Ministry of Forests, Lands and Natural Resource Operations, accessed July 22, 2021, env.gov.bc.ca/fw/wildlife/management-issues/docs/grey_wolf_management_plan.pdf.

"Managing Raccoon Pests," Province of British Columbia, accessed July 22, 2021, gov.bc.ca/gov/content/environment/pesticides-pest-management/managing-pests/animals/raccoons.

"New Grizzly Bear Regulations—Results," govTogetherBC, accessed July 22, 2021, engage.gov.bc.ca/govtogetherbc/impact/new-grizzly-bear-regulations-results/.

"Raccoons," PAWS, accessed July 22, 2021, paws.org/resources/raccoons/.

"River Otter," Sierra Club BC, accessed July 22, 2021, sierraclub.bc.ca/river-otter/.

Strandberg, Diane. "Anmore couple rescues bear cub but faces BC Conservation investigation," *Times Colonist, Tri-City News*, January 10, 2020, timescolonist.com/2.2551/2.5666/anmore-couple-rescues-bear-cub-but-faces-bc-conservation-investigation-1.24050464.

"Sylvilagus floridanus eastern cottontail," Animal Diversity Web, University of Michigan, accessed July 22, 2021, animaldiversity.org/accounts/Sylvilagus_floridanus/.

"Teaching Otters to Swim," Critter Care, accessed July 22, 2021, crittercare-wildlife.org/teaching-otters-to-swim.

"Trapping Regulations," Ministry of Environment and Climate Change Strategy, accessed July 22, 2021, env.gov.bc.ca/wld/documents/trapping_regulations.pdf.

"What to do if you Find a Deer Fawn," BC SPCA, accessed July 22, 2021,
spca.bc.ca/wp-content/uploads/baby-deer-2014-rack-card.pdf.

"Wildlife Act," Province of British Columbia, accessed July 22, 2021, bclaws.
gov.bc.ca/civix/document/id/complete/statreg/96488_01#section21.

ORGANIZATIONS THAT CARE FOR SICK, INJURED, OR ORPHANED ANIMALS IN BC

Critter Care Wildlife Society | crittercarewildlife.org

Northern Lights Wildlife Shelter | wildlifeshelter.com

The Fur-bearers | thefurbearers.com

Grouse Mountain Refuge for Endangered Wildlife | grousemountain.com/
wildlife-refuge

Marine Mammal Rescue | vanaqua.org/marine-mammal-rescue

North Island Wildlife Recovery Centre | niwra.org

To find see if there's an animal rehabilitator near you, check out wrnbc.org/
contact/find-a-local-rehabilitator/

RECOMMENDED RESOURCES

If you want to learn more about wild animal rehabilitation and conservation, here are a few helpful resources:

BC Wildlife Park Kamloops: What to do if you've found injured wild-
life | bcwildlife.org/injuredwildlife.htm

Conservation Officer Service | gov.bc.ca/gov/content/environment/
natural-resource-stewardship/natural-resource-law-enforcement/
conservation-officer-service

Wild Safe BC: Reducing Conflict Where We Play | wildsafebc.com/
learn/play

The Province of British Columbia: Human-Wildlife Conflict | gov.bc.ca/
gov/content/environment/plants-animals-ecosystems/wildlife/
human-wildlife-conflict

BC Wildlife Federation | bcwf.bc.ca

British Columbia Conservation Foundation | bccf.com

Raincoast Conservation Foundation | raincoast.org

INDEX